King of a Rainy Country

King of a Rainy Country

MATTHEW SWEENEY

2018

Published by Arc Publications
Nanholme Mill, Shaw Wood Road,
Todmorden OL14 6DA, UK
www.arcpublications.co.uk

Copyright © Estate of Matthew Sweeney, 2018
Copyright in the present edition © Arc Publications, 2018
Design by Tony Ward
Printed by TJ International, Padstow, Cornwall

978 1911469 52 0 (pbk)
978 1911469 53 7 (hbk)
978 1911469 54 4 (ebk)

Cover illustration:
Gustave Doré *Les Saltimbanques* (1874), oil on canvas
Musée d'art Roger-Quilliot, Clermont-Ferrand

ACKNOWLEDGEMENTS
Thanks are due to the editors of the
following publications in which some of these
pieces have already appeared:
*Blackbox Manifold, The High Window, The Penny Dreadful,
PN Review, Poetry, Poetry Review, The Wolf.*

Editor for the UK and Ireland:
John Wedgewood Clarke

For Mary,
who brought me to Paris

Je suis comme le roi d'un pays pluvieux,
Riche, mais impuissant, jeune et pourtant très vieux,
Qui, de ses précepteurs méprisant les courbettes,
S'ennuie avec ses chiens comme avec d'autres bêtes.
Rien ne peut l'égayer, ni gibier, ni faucon,
Ni son peuple mourant en face du balcon.

from *Les Fleurs du Mal,* LXXVII
CHARLES BAUDELAIRE

Banquo: It will be rain to-night.
First Murderer: Let it come down.

from *Macbeth, Act III, Scene III*
WILLIAM SHAKESPEARE

CONTENTS

I spent some months in Paris during the first half of 2016. While there I set myself the task of responding in a series of prose poems to the edgy city Paris had become, while bouncing off Baudelaire's posthumously published collection of prose poems, *Le Spleen de Paris.* Anyone who knows these will agree they read very differently to Baudelaire's celebrated poems collected in *Les Fleurs du Mal.* In fact, at first sight, it's hard to see how the prose things are poems at all. Baudelaire's own description of them was *petits poèmes en prose.* This doesn't mean that he went for a heightened or poetic prose. No, there's nothing poetic about these prose poems. And the range of the fifty of them in the sequence is wide – sometimes they're little stories or parables, other times meditations or epiphanies. They can simply be rants or paeans, or slightly extended japes, and yes, frequently they're funny, which his regular poems never are. Anyway, I was immediately taken with them – I'd never read them before I went to live in Paris. I could see they were nothing like the contemporary prose poem (however one might define that), which in the main has come into existence via the USA (and which I've never been wildly enamoured of). Anyway, I took the decision to model my efforts as much as I could on Baudelaire's pieces, and strive for as wide a range as possible. Reading his, I never knew what was coming next, and I wanted some of the same effect. Sometimes I stayed quite close to Baudelaire, so that the result could be seen as a translation, almost, or at least a version. Other times, I tried to come up with something original, but very much along the lines of something Baudelaire had done. And there was a third category where I felt I was entering into dialogue with Baudelaire (*'Pied-Noir'* included in *PN Review 238,* Vol. 44 No. 2, Nov-Dec 2017 would be one of those) – the piece in itself might bear no resemblance to any of his prose poems, but might be written in a way that was appropriate to how he'd operated. I did not attempt, or feel able, to respond to all of Baudelaire's prose poems (for a start, he was frequently misogynistic, which made me wary) but I endeavoured to cover as much of his sequence as possible, and to have in the end fifty pieces in my own sequence, as well.

Matthew Sweeney

So many people in Paris seem to be mad.
They smile at you, and stare into your eyes
on the Métro. They brush up against you
in the supermarket queue, as if they don't
see you're there. They stand on the street
and shout at no one that's visible, and they
keep shrieking on till you've shrunk away.
Even their dogs live on their own planet.
I've bought Baudelaire's Le Spleen de Paris
in translation, hoping that (even at this
distance in time) it'll offer a guide to this
weird city that used to be his. That still is.
And I'll study it well, and learn how to
negotiate the rapids of no line-breaks, no
easy rhymes, no verse-rhythms, then I'll
become a modern version of that flâneur
he was, and go out with my yellow notebook,
my green pen, and maybe I'll find a response.

I. THE BOTTLE-GATHERER

'Bottle-gatherer, what do you hope to gain from this gathering of the discards of other people's merry-making, beyond the few cents you'll accrue?'

'I will enjoy the echo of their celebrating. And besides, the giant snake-head of the bottle-bank is at least a block away. I am helping them.'

'And does that offer you a pleasure in these days of random mass shootings in bars and music venues?'

'Any bottle that has drops of wine in it and no drops of blood pleases me.'

'Do you believe in God, my friend?'

'I am not your friend, good Sir, although I wish you well. And I'll need at least a year to answer your question.'

'Fine then, tell me do you differentiate between green, brown and colourless bottles?'

'No more than the skin-colours or hair-colours of our citizens.'

'Can I help you, for no recompense, to bring the bottles to the big metal snake?'

'Ah, kind sir, I thank you, but some journeys are better taken alone.'

Wanting a brioche for breakfast, I took the back street with the hippy murals. The sky was dull but dry. Approaching me was a woman with a child and carrying what had to be a ukulele in a small black case. I hurried on, calculating which *boulangerie* would be the best bet.

As I entered the chosen one, a beggar on the pavement was shouting, not at me, not at anybody. A black poodle was waiting at the door. I emerged with the half bread / half cake and remembered I needed coffee and grape juice, so I veered for Carrefour. The yellow sign with the name was lit up like a lighthouse beam dimmed by fog. I found my two items, added a third – *confiture figues violettes*. At the check-out I realised I had insufficient cash so I eased my card into the machine. A jolly young dark-bearded man queued behind me was engaged in cheerful banter with the cashier. They were both laughing. I bustled my new belongings into a plastic bag and scuttled out of the supermarket.

I nearly ran into a soldier in camouflage uniform with a black machine gun nestling in his arms. What was he doing here? I felt like I was back on the streets of Derry in the '70s. I stood aside to let him walk on, but he was in no hurry. I knew it would be bad luck to march past him. Apart from anything else, that machine gun could go off accidentally. I remembered stories about it having happened before.

When eventually I got halfway up the street the young man from the supermarket came running after me – *votre carte, monsieur. Merci*, I said, *merci*, as he walked away. I realised that if it hadn't been for the soldier, I'd have been gone from sight, and would have no idea of what had happened to my card. Just then I heard faint music that had to be emanating from a ukulele. Each plucked note seemed to drop from the cloudy sky. They all seemed slightly out of tune.

3. POMMES SAUTÉES

As I walked up the Rue des Martyrs with my bag of small, perfect, waxy potatoes I doffed my imaginary hat to Monsieur Parmentier. Well, I do have a hat and wore it a lot not so long ago to cover a healing wound on my forehead but this wasn't necessary anymore, and anyway the hat wasn't with me now in Paris. Nor was Monsieur Parmentier, though any remains of him lie in a plot in Père-Lachaise ringed by potato plants.

I would not be intending to cook my potatoes but for the duplicitous actions of Parmentier back in the late years of the eighteenth century. After he'd realised that this odd-shaped tuber looted from the Incas in Peru (along with their gold and silver) was extremely nutritious, and no one would believe him, he'd come up with a ruse. Using money given to him by King Louis XVI he purchased a plot of impoverished ground outside Paris, in Neuilly-sur-Seine, and planted it with potatoes. When the time to dig them came, he built a fence around them and put armed guards outside it. These men wore uniforms the colour of potatoes. They were told to leak the news that they were guarding an extremely precious food. Then, one night, they left their post. Thieves arrived within a couple of hours and stole the entire crop. Over the next few days the potatoes were sold in the city's markets as the food of kings.

So my guests wouldn't know they would be eating the food of kings. Nor would I tell them, though I might well concoct a story about the breed of pigs their pork chops had come from. And the posh wine that had yielded the wine vinegar I'd used in the salad dressing. I could try telling them I'd climbed over the fence of Père-Lachaise the previous night, armed with a phone-torch, a trowelling spade and a canvas bag, and dug the potatoes from Monsieur Parmentier's plot – only taking the small ones that were right for *pommes sautées*, of course – but I know they wouldn't believe me.

I was distracted from these smug reveries by my mobile phone ringing. I dug it out of my pocket and answered it, thinking one advantage of being in France was that nobody rang me. The voice at the other end was not one I recognised. It said, at first quietly 'Are you ok?', then in a louder voice, 'Please tell me you're ok over there', and that was it. When I went to check the number, it had been withheld. What had I landed myself in, I wondered? I went home to deal with my nineteenth-century French meal.

4. HASHISH

It is a Saturday morning, not early. The Parisians are shopping – pulling big bags on wheels behind them, filling these with enough vegetables and fruit to feed a football team. As I leave the *boulangerie* with my croissants I pass a man with downcast eyes, an Indian-looking blanket wrapped like a cape around him, and his bare feet the dirtiest I have ever seen. I look away and turn into Rue Choron.

I immediately detect a strong smell of marijuana, and see a grey-bearded man sitting on a pile of clothes on the pavement. He is sucking on a joint. I look around for any sign of the armed police but they're not here. Maybe something like this is no longer on their agenda. I remember when I first encountered marijuana – what was then more commonly called hashish, or hash. I was a student in Dublin and my fellow-student flatmates were partakers, but I was a resister. I believed they were shamming, that nothing was happening when they smoked their conical joints. Certainly nothing was happening with me. So one Sunday afternoon, after the latest failure, I stormed out, muttering, and for some reason ended up in the nearby small church which I'd never entered before. A mass was taking place. I sat there feeling weirdly serene, and suddenly I noticed the priest had huge owl eyes. His priestly robes had become psychedelic with throbbing colours, and I wasn't smelling but drinking the incense which tasted like nectar. And the ceremony of the mass became more like an Aztec sacrificial ritual. I had a bit of apologising to do to the boys when I got back to the flat.

Monsieur Baudelaire held out a bit longer, though. Oh, he occasionally showed up at the regular group-meetings in the Île St-Louis that came to be called *Club des Hashichins* but he rarely partook of the drug (which was consumed in a thick greenish soup or jam, mixed with coffee, ground pistachio, cloves, nutmeg and cinnamon, and sugar). In fact, he was scornfully dismissive of it, preferring by far wine. 'Wine exalts the will', he wrote, 'hashish annihilates it.' If my French was good enough I'd convey that sentiment to the man sitting on the clothes, smoking the joint, but first I'd have to go to Carrefour and buy him a half-decent bottle of wine and a corkscrew.

This morning Rue Hippolyte Lebas is closed to cars. A yellow sign has in large black letters the message *Voie Réservée aux Cyclistes et aux Piétons de 10H à 14H*, and a policeman and a policewoman are standing in front of it, ensuring the sign is obeyed. I walk past them to a Rue des Martyrs that is more crowded than usual. People are standing about in small groups, as if awaiting some diversion. Dotted at intervals all along the street are small tables holding bunches of tiny white flowers swaddled in green leaves that are for sale – lily of the valley, it seems. Of course, this is Mayday – in Paris *La Fête du Muguet*. The road is closed off because of a workers' march, no doubt, and that's what the flock of people are waiting for. France had no Margaret Thatcher to emasculate the unions.

The queue leading into the *artisan pâtissier* is long and moving slowly, but the sun is shining. Most people emerge with pastries or cakes in white cardboard boxes. Then I glimpse more police – three males, this time, each of them cradling a machine gun. They are walking close to the shop entrances in a way that resembles hunters moving over the veldt. Oh, I hope they get what they're after, or foil what other people are planning to do, misguided people, brainwashed people, bad people. Is there anything worse than the fanatic mindset? And all done in the name of religion, too. Last time I was in London I met a friend in a Pakistani restaurant in Whitechapel and he informed me he was founding a new religion based on dinosaur ghosts. When I reacted with laughter he got angry, and said I'd be wanting to convert to his religion when it was up and running. Whatever about this, I couldn't see my friend ever planting bombs or going on shooting sprees in the name of his religion. Maybe I should phone him up to say I will join him in his venture, become one of his priests, even. What kind of vestments has he in mind? What kind of rites does he envisage taking place, and what kind of building might house this religion of his? Will there be vows to take? I regret not having been more interested when he told me about his development. I need to get back to London and see him again.

In the meantime I must go and buy a couple of small bunches of the tiny white flowers and take them back to the old-fashioned flat in the building designed by Haussmann. The lift is working again and will whisk me up to the fourth floor.

The bunches of the lily of the valley flowers are like miniature cousins of the bunch of white roses on the mantelpiece. Each have their guardians of green. I feel blessed by flowers.

Paris is a place where one can trust in the growers of plants to deliver what's right. No wonder Monsieur Baudelaire was proud to be a Parisian. I am haughtily grateful to have French blood on my mother's side – her maiden name was Lavelle, and once in Paris I tried to trace the family tree back as far as I could go. I was compromised somewhat by the French Revolution. The people in the records centre couldn't be exact, but I was told my ancestor had been a soldier who'd sailed from La Rochelle on the expedition to liberate Ireland from the English (known in Ireland as the Year of the French), and his ship had run aground in a storm on the shores of Mayo. He'd clearly been fortunate to meet an Irish lassie, rather than an Irish spear, otherwise I wouldn't be writing this. I have to say I find it hard to imagine having an ancestor who was a soldier. I have never had any gift for fighting – even when I was bullied at boarding school I stood passively when the blows pummelled down from the fists of the chief bully. Oh, my grandfather was from Mayo and cooked French stuff during my childhood, which disconcerted my little friends at primary school.

I am ashamed that my command of the French language is so awful. I have tried to learn the language – I did one year at secondary school in Donegal when I was still too young to go to the boarding school my father had earmarked me for. I remember little about that year of French except the priest who taught us (who later became the Bishop of Derry) had two straps for punishing us boys, one soft one he called *madame*, one tougher one he called *monsieur*.

Someone once suggested that if I undertook a rigorous

course of hypnotism my inherited French would come spouting out of me, all rolled *r*'s and *z* noises, but I couldn't take the fellow whose theory this was seriously. I once enrolled in a French evening class in London but the pathetic French I had was better than what most of the rest of the class had, so progress was slow – and was not helped by my missing half the classes. Maybe I should go to Fnac and invest in a CD of *Teach Yourself French*, then go and spend the afternoons in a lively bar, taking off the headphones from time to time to ingest the atmo and add to my rapidly improving French some Parisian slang. It's the least a person with French blood who's living in Paris for a time should do.

As I walked down Rue de Maubeuge today on my way to Boulevard Haussmann and Galeries Lafayette I encountered three soldiers in full camouflage uniform (even their rucksacks were in camouflage) stalking along with machine guns. Two of them were black, one white. A little boy (who looked Arab), accompanied by his mother, waved and cheered at them. The soldiers smiled shyly back, then resumed their surveying of the street.

It occurred to me that in the event of these soldiers having occasion to open fire (Lord preserve this from happening) that little boy might be in danger of getting accidentally shot. Wasn't it called collateral damage – a horribly distant and impersonal word for what it would be describing? This is obviously a new term, as the meaning is not included among the definitions of the word in my *Collins Concise English Dictionary*. Maybe it's come into English from French.

I suddenly saw my distant ancestor, the soldier who ended up in Mayo in 1798, walking along these Parisian streets. His uniform would be quite different to this modern camouflage stuff. No, I see him in a blue jacket with red epaulettes and cuffs, and white breeches. On his head is a tricorn hat with a tricolour cockade. His weapon is not a machine-gun as these are not available yet, no, in his hands is a muzzle-loading musket – probably a .69 calibre Charleville. Everybody is cheering him. I join in and try to communicate with him but of course my French is not good enough for him to understand.

I have reached Boulevard Haussmann now and have to push my way through hordes of Japanese tourists on the pavement. To my amazement and no little irritation (although I have nothing against Japanese people and greatly enjoyed my one visit to their country), Galeries Lafayette is thronging with Japanese. There must be more of them here than on the island of Hokkaido. I notice that the department store even offers a 'Japan Welcome' facility, and some of the serving assistants speak Japanese. I sniff around the trendy French trainers' section, Geox, but it is too crowded, so I head for the food hall instead. This involves leaving the building I am in, crossing Avenue Haussmann, and entering another building of the vast Galeries Lafayette emporium.

For a cook it is a bit like entering heaven. As well as the food on display, there is all the kitchen equipment a professional cook could wish for. I find the meat department and buy a *faux filet* steak, then a punnet of thin little potatoes that are perfect for sautéing, and a green and purple lettuce. And on the way out a baguette, of course, but only after taking the escalator to the first floor and *La Cave* which has the best wine selection in the world. I walk slowly along the shelves drooling at the wines that are displayed, region by region, sometimes (the famous Bordeaux producers, for example), wine by wine. I content myself with a couple of bottles from the South West that are at the cheaper end of the spectrum.

Walking back down Boulevard Haussmann I am laden down with a heavy, sturdy paper bag in each hand, each emblazoned with the logo of Galeries Lafayette. I am beginning to get hungry and start envisioning the full plate I will place in front of me. At that moment three more soldiers in camouflage uniform, carrying machine guns, walk past me and cross the street, two white men and one black this time. One of the white soldiers bears a striking resemblance to my grandfather from photographs at home showing him young and in the uniform of the Royal Irish Constabulary.

That night I couldn't sleep. I kept seeing soldiers, they were walking along every street in Paris. They could see in the dark. They could fly – I watched three of them drift across the face of the moon. One shot at it, a quick *rat-tat-tat* from his machine gun that downed a bat who was in the wrong place at the very wrong time. Another fired his musket at an owl – he missed the first time, but muzzle-loaded again twice within a minute and finally downed the big-eyed nocturnal bird, whose corpse fell on the sleeping head of a homeless man, who jumped to his feet, shouting.

I felt like a cognac but had none, so I opened a bottle of nondescript Bordeaux. I also, for some reason, peeled a baby onion and chewed it raw, then swallowed the pieces. Was that the explosion of a bomb I heard faintly from far across the city? I switched on my iPad and looked at the breaking news but there was no report of a bomb, in Paris or anywhere. I slipped a CD of Ali Farka Touré into my laptop.

I opened the shutters and took my glass of wine out onto the balcony. I leant over and looked down at the Rue Rodier which was more or less empty – apart from a couple who were being too public with their intimate activity. 'Baudelaire, are you there?', I whispered into the not quite dark. 'I need some guidance on how to continue responding to all this.' At that, the sky took on a slight lavender hue, the moon seemed to revolve, two stars fell into the Atlantic or the Mediterranean, I couldn't say which, and a dog howled somewhere up in Montmartre. If I didn't know better I'd say I was stoned on marijuana, or that Baudelaire was, despite his being in the land of the dead, and not having had any time for the stuff. Ali Farka Touré's njarka sawed away like an aural dancing snake in the room behind me.

I poured myself another glass of the red wine. I'd heard no further sound of what might be explosions or no further shooting, and the soldiers had left the sky, which had resumed its normal colour. There was half a cooked beetroot in the fridge which I picked up, ground pepper onto, and devoured, then washed the red from my fingers. I lay down on the sofa and looked at the ceiling. For some reason I'd have welcomed seeing a large spider up there. Or hearing a mouse rustling about in the corner of the room. I thought of the white, albino mouse I'd kept as a pet, that I'd given the name of Luigi to, and that I'd let go up one sleeve and down the other, emerging with his pink eyes flashing. My mother had hated that little creature. She'd called it a rat. Once when I went off to the Gaeltacht in Ranafast for three weeks, she starved the mouse and I came back to find it shrivelled and dead. Murderer!

Why were these memories coming back to me? Was it the armed policemen and soldiers I kept seeing on the streets? Was it the still shocking news of those who'd been gunned down, or blown up by the fanatics in November 2015? I sat back and tried to let the music wash over me. Once I'd seen Ali Farke Touré play live in the South Bank Centre in London and I'd never forget it. I poured one more glass of the wine and put the cork in the bottle.

I'm not talking about Neuilly anymore. Monsieur Parmentier is long dead and potatoes are everywhere. I'm not including *banlieues aisées* in this.

I'm only considering *banlieues défavorisées*. Like Clichy-Sous-Bois. Where the rodeos happened long ago in 1981. Cars stolen, stunt driving, races, cars abandoned, set on fire.

And in 2005, the riots where hundreds of youths stood against the police. It got on the news all over the world. Were these youths French? Or Arab? Or neither? What were they, then?

So when the agents of Isis came snooping, these youths might have been ripe for recruiting, for brainwashing. For fanaticising.

Prisons are apparently the best recruiting grounds.

When one feels one is nothing and a stranger says you can be a big something, even if it will cost you your life, you listen. It might take a few tellings. What is life worth, after all, if all one knows is one's *banlieue*?

I saw a powerful film that touched on the subject at the 2016 Cork French Film Festival. The film was called *Dheepan* and concerned a Sri Lankan family, or apparent family, who'd come to live in a tower block in one of the *banlieues*. The man had taken the job of caretaker of the estate.

Or part of the estate, because it quickly became apparent that sections of the estate had different bosses. And these bosses were brutal – as brutal and final as the IRA in Belfast or the Mafia in New York. And that drugs and drug-money was in the background.

Which is not certainly the case with Isis, although I have read convincing evidence. Opinions differ, though.

What is sure is that Isis agents come, trying to persuade these young men and women to accompany them to Syria for training, then return to Paris to set off bombs in places like the Stade de France, where France were playing football against the old enemy Germany, or to shoot people in theatres like the Bataclan, or in bars like the *Café Bonne Bière* and *Le Carillon* on the Canal St-Martin.

What is Paris and the world coming to? I think Baudelaire would be truly appalled.

When I went out into Rue Rodier this morning, there was a short, baldish, mad woman screeching at all and sundry as she walked up the middle of the road. Is this how the day begins, I asked myself. I decided there and then I had to go to the Cimetière du Montparnasse and stand in front of Baudelaire's grave. These long-distance attempts at communicating with him weren't working too well.

I eventually found the grave. It wasn't the grandest, I'd have to say. An off-white tombstone rising from a cement grey-and-white horizontal stone that I'd call cramped, and yes, scruffy. Not what I'd expected for arguably France's best-ever poet. On the tombstone, among other names, Charles Baudelaire, *à l'âge 46 ans, le 31 août 1867.* Far too young, really. It didn't mention that he'd died of syphilis. On the flat stone loads of flowers, red mainly, a preponderance of roses. Some of these were withered. There were also, oddly enough, a number of Métro tickets, a 20 cent coin, and a cigarette. And little stones, too angular to be called pebbles. And there were at least three scribbled notes. Two of these were in French, the third in English. I copied down what it said – *I wait for a burning dreamland, a temple in flames, come the unknown* (the commas are mine). Were these lines of Baudelaire's in translation? (I stuck them into Google when I got back but the search yielded nothing.) Or were they a message for me? I was intending to ask him what was going to happen in France, and if there was any way I should be responding in what I was writing. If this was his answer, it was a pretty gloomy one. I verbalised my question to him, suddenly unaware if he'd understood English or not. No answer came back in any language. I did a sort of a genuflection and walked slowly away.

As I was here, I decided also to pay homage to Beckett. I'd once found his grave before and had left a note on it – *Godot here, where the fuck are you?* This time I had difficulty locating it, but I did. The dates were 1906-1989. A longer stint of life. No tombstone, but a more refined flat stone, in grey speckled marble. Beckett would have found these times troubled too.

I remembered the Peruvian poet, César Vallejo, used to lie here. His most famous poem opened with the line *I will die in Paris in the rain*. It had been raining the day I went looking for his grave, and in my search I kept meeting a Peruvian couple on the same quest. Eventually it was explained to us that a week previously the Peruvian authorities had exhumed Vallejo's remains for reburial in Lima. At least Baudelaire was still here. I was glad I'd come to see him.

I went to sleep quickly that night but woke in the small hours. It was no noise that had woken me but I was soon so wide-awake I knew I would get no more sleep. And now I heard a very low sound, the clink of a glass against a bottle. I got out of bed and tweaked the curtains open. There, seated at the round red table on the balcony, was a very handsome man, his black hair with a reddish tint swept back from his forehead. He smiled and beckoned me to the empty chair opposite him.

I pulled on my kimono and went out to join him. His beauty was quite androgynous – not really David Bowie or Prince, but getting there. Indeed, he looked like one of the lords of rock music. He was dressed in a purple suit with a shiny mauve, open-necked shirt. I was startled to see that the tiny figures dangling from his ears on silver chains were human and squirmingly alive, and their pointed back teeth showed me they were diminutive vampires. Well, well, well, I thought. Who have we here?

'Can I pour you a glass of wine?', my new companion said. 'I think you'll like it. It's a 2005 St-Estèphe.'

'Absolutely', I said. I'd never had a top St-Estèphe before.

'Please allow me to introduce myself', the man said, 'My name is Adramelech.'

'That's an unusual name.'

'Yes, it means "King of Fire".'

I focused on the black rose with red edges in his top buttonhole. Of course.

'Has Monsieur Baudelaire sent you?'

'Ah, Charles. *Les Fleurs du Mal* – a book that is valued highly where I come from.'

'I suppose so', I said.

I belatedly became aware of his eyes – they resembled violets still heavy with the rain from a storm. One could drown in them, but I saw two little films there, neither of which I liked at all. The first showed a young curly-haired man concealing a machine gun inside a long black overcoat and boarding a crowded Métro train. The second showed a young woman with very short hair strapping a bomb-vest on her, then closing a denim jacket on top, before also taking the Métro.

'You are appalled by what you see?'

'Yes, I am. We all are, apart from maybe you – and them. You must be able to stop them. What can I do to make you do this?'

'Ah, stop them? That might prove difficult. They are doing what they're doing for God, not for a lowly devil like me. Can I pour you more wine?'

I nodded, at a loss for how to continue. The devil smiled at me, flashing his teeth.

'As to what you can do? You might try to write a slightly different kind of poetry. I've read a couple of your books. You tend to sit on the fence, don't you?'

I was immediately reminded of an occasion in London in the late 1980s when I was approached in a bar in Notting Hill Gate by a couple of IRA men who tried to tell me something similar. They put their point more clearly, and were a lot ruder, if not downright contemptuous.

'And if I did manage to start writing in a way that was more to your liking', I said, 'would you take steps to try to dissuade the jihadist murderers?'

He laughed.

'I've already told you I can have little influence in the matter of God. One time maybe, not now. Would you like to help me finish the wine? I could spirit up another bottle of it but I think we've spoken enough.'

'Yes, I agree,' I said.

He threw the wine into him and this time I noticed that the two tiny vampires hanging from his ears took an interest, as if they sometimes were gifted a drop of the dregs, despite it being the wrong red liquid. Then, in front of me, he disappeared, as quickly and as completely as the ghost of my grandfather had disappeared when he'd come to me three days after he'd died.

I slowly sipped the rest of the wine, then took the devil's glasses and empty bottle into the kitchen. I climbed back into bed and made a vain attempt to drift back again into the cleansing world of sleep.

After all that albeit indirect contact with Monsieur Baudelaire, I decided I had to revisit one of his old haunts, Pigalle. I could walk there fairly easily – up to the top of Rue des Martyrs onto Boulevard de Clichy. This led to Place Pigalle, beyond which lay the locale I was after. At first sight, it appeared much like it would have looked in Baudelaire's time. All the sex shops were still there. Doubtlessly the brothels were lurking behind them. Was it here that Baudelaire had picked up his syphilis? Then I noticed that one sex shop was proudly announcing its existence since 1978, while another advertised itself as a *Supermarché Érotique*, so maybe these were not the old nineteenth-century establishments, given repeated facelifts. Maybe the place had even been cleaned up during the twentieth century, only to come back later as a kind of tourist nostalgia. I didn't imagine the majority of the clientele were French these days.

As I continued along the Boulevard I noticed that groups of mainly black and Arab men were sitting on seats in the bush-lined promenade in the middle of the street. It made sense on such a sunny day. I spied just ahead of me what remains of the famous nineteenth-century cabaret, *Le Chat Noir*, still famous because of Steinlein's iconic poster art. I stood there, imagining myself pitching up one evening in the 1880s and seating myself at a table with Toulouse-Lautrec and Aristide Bruant. I carried on, and, after Rue Lepic, I came across the Moulin Rouge. It looked somewhat tawdry now. I figured that Baudelaire would have trotted along to see the can-can dancers, but he was not sadly around in 1882 to witness Joseph Pujol, Monsieur le Pétomane, play 'O Sole Mio' on an ocarina through a rubber tube in his anus at the celebrated nightspot.

I passed a bistro called *Le Sanglier Bleu* under the picture of a blue boar. This appealed to me, as the Sweeney coat of arms sported three wild boars, and when I'd been a student in Freiburg, in the Black Forest, in the late 1970s, wild boar had often appeared on the menu. I'd even written a piece imagining turning into a boar.

For variety I took a different route back – down Rue de Douai. I came to Place André Breton. He'd possibly been my dead poet friend John Hartley Williams's hero, so I'd have to stop here for a drink. I sat on the *terrasse* of a bar and ordered a small glass of red *vin du moment*. As I sipped it, trying to block out the rap that was playing, I noticed an incident happening several metres away. Four policemen, all wearing sunglasses, were standing round a young black man at a motorcycle. One of the policemen was on the phone. Then an Arab man arrived and engaged in conversation with this policeman, showing him documents. Was this a thwarted theft, I began to wonder? The young black man was now gesticulating vehemently. A police-car arrived with what seemed to be a sergeant who handcuffed and arrested the black man, putting him into the backseat of the car which drove away. I finished my drink, paid and walked on.

In the last bit of Rue de Douai more or less every shop sold guitars. There were all kinds here, electric and acoustic, all kinds of prices. I suddenly wondered if Baudelaire could play the guitar at all. I found myself being severely tempted by the ukuleles. They were cheap – a 100 euros or less. I'd heard they were easy enough to learn. And they were eminently portable. A cute red one caught my eye particularly. I decided I'd think about it, and walked on.

I was soon back in Rue des Martyrs where I bought a baguette in a *pâtisserie* and came out to two police vans parking, then disgorging policemen with machine guns. Paris had not been like this last time I'd been here, but then things had happened.

13. THE SCORPION

I needed something different in the food line so I opted to go for Chinese. I headed for Belleville, which I knew was the second Chinatown, or *Quartier Chinois*, in Paris but a friend who'd lived some years in Shanghai, then moved to Paris, had recommended a place. It wouldn't stand out from the restaurants around it, he said, but it was worth making a small effort to find. The name was *Wen Zhou*, but I should know there were two restaurants with that name, and the one I was looking for had *Chez Alex* in brackets after it. I soon saw this, but only after suffering the embarrassment of going into the wrong one first.

It was not that crowded. I was directed to a table by a window. I scanned the wine-list, ordered a bottle of Muscadet *sur lie*, then turned to the food choices. This was not easy – so much on the menu looked enticing. I had a sure feeling I'd been directed to a good place.

By the time the wine came I'd made my choice – smoked duck, and aubergine with minced beef. I knew these two dishes from a good Chinese in London, and if they were half as good here, they'd be very welcome. I also liked the look of crab with ginger and spring onion, but I didn't want to order too much – anyway the crab might very well come in the shell, which I knew from experience would be very messy. I wanted egg-fried rice but hadn't a clue how to ask for that, so I went for steamed rice. I did manage to convey that I wanted a bowl and chopsticks.

I poured a glass of wine and surveyed the room. Something two tables away caught my attention – it was a scorpion walking along the table top. The creature seemed be on a blue string acting as a lead. This was held by a very cheeky looking blond-haired boy who was greatly enjoying my interest in his pet. So was the boy's companion, clearly his father as their features chimed. This man looked like a not-so-ex-hippy, or maybe a performer of some nature.

The boy put a prawn on the table and allowed the scorpion to approach it.

I had no idea scorpions were ever kept as pets. I knew they did exist in France, in the south, if not in Paris. I remembered having been on holiday in Bouzigues, south of Sète, in the '70s and opening the door of the rented house to find it crawling with scorpions. I would never forget the image of their scuttling here and there, with those sinister, stinging tails curved above them. I don't remember how we got rid of the bulk of them but I do recall my killing the last one by drowning it in a bowl of pure alcohol from a bottle I'd found under the sink. I'd kept the corpse as a trophy, protected by cotton wool in a matchbox, for years, until the thing had disintegrated.

Now I was looking at a scorpion's menacing tail again. I noticed another slightly younger boy, at a different table, was also captivated. He had brought a toy with him, a kind of robot soldier that had probably cost a lot and would kill the scorpion if pitted against it, but its owner had lost interest in it. He wanted the scorpion.

Reluctantly I turned my attention to my food which turned out to be excellent, especially the aubergine (how could the Chinese get their aubergine so soft?). As I savoured my meal, I noticed the scorpion boy leaving with his father, without having seen what he'd done with his arachnid. I noticed the other boy looking after him as they exited the door.

Because Baudelaire loved the circus I wanted to see one in Paris, and I wanted, if possible, to see one he might have seen. The obvious one, after a bit of research, was the *Cirque d'Hiver* which started in 1852 (called then *Cirque Napoléon*), so he might very well have visited it. In fact, given his predilection for the circus and all such activities, I could be sure he'd been there.

What could I find out about the *Cirque d'Hiver*? The first thing I had to rule out was that it wasn't just a winter circus, given the name. Apparently not, but the bad news was that the next run of performances were in Le Havre. Did I want to go enough to take a train to Normandy, and pay for a night in a hotel there? Baudelaire certainly wouldn't have seen it in Le Havre. It probably didn't travel anywhere back then.

And I wanted to know what animals were left performing in the circus, if any. When I'd lived in London I'd witnessed the shocking development of animal-free circuses. I have never wanted animals to suffer, but the memory I had of circuses coming to Donegal in my childhood, with satanic monkeys, terrifying tigers, solitary lions, remained very powerful to me. Those animals had not seemed mistreated. I had never been too thrilled by the clowns or the tightrope walkers. It was the circus animals that had excited me. I couldn't find out much about what I'd see in Le Havre.

I suddenly remembered that the wonderful Elizabeth Bishop had penned a poem called 'Cirque d'Hiver'. I tracked it down, and re-read it, for the first time in years. It was charming, and beautifully made, as one might expect, but it was slightly alarming. It depicted the movement of a mechanical toy – a little circus horse, with real white hair, with a little dancer on his back, both pierced by a stake that turned into a big metal key beneath the horse. It didn't hold

40

out much hope for seeing real animals.

I decided I needed to go to Rue Amelot to see the building of the *Cirque d'Hiver Bouglione*, as it's known since the Bouglione family took it over. I wanted to see it as I'd never seen a circus that didn't take place in a tent. The building was apparently an oval polygon with twenty sides, and Corinthian columns at the angles, but no tent pole. Baudelaire would have loved it.

Today I've been invited to an *atelier* – a painter's studio. I don't know the artist. She's an Argentinian woman who's lived in Paris a long time, and is a friend of friends of mine. They thought I'd be interested. They don't even know that I'm thinking of calling my next poetry collection *My Life as a Painter*. Have I ever been a painter? Of course not. Poems thrive on lies – I see poetry as a kind of lying oneself to the truth.

I know nothing about her work but I'll find out. I take the Métro to Gare de L'Est and walk the rest of the way to the Canal Saint-Martin. I know this area slightly. An American poet friend of mine, C. K. Williams (now sadly dead), used to live here.

I come to the canal, walk across a bridge and keep going. Soon I come to the Carillon bar where a number of young people lost their lives in the November 2015 shootings. Such a terrible thing. I had been wondering why the terrorists had targeted this area but a local resident enlightened me. When he'd moved there, in the late '80s, he said, it had been predominately a Kabyle Algerian district but then, with gentrification, the Algerians had gradually moved out. It was certainly pretty bo-bo here now.

I walk back to the canal. I see little yachts manoeuvring about in the still water, then notice three men standing on the canal-bank with remote controls. Grown men with toys – why not? There are a few other men fishing, although what they'd catch here is a good question. And there are loads of young people with bottles of beer or wine.

I meet my friends and the artist in a bar. We have one drink and make our way to the studio. This turns out to be through a courtyard with plants, then up a staircase. Paintings are on the walls, and drawings are piled up on a table, separated by sheets of transparent paper. I'm happy to say I like the work, particularly the paintings.

They're strange – abstract, with the ghosts of concrete scenes lurking behind them. As if a scene was painted then deliberately lost or buried. I think if I was a painter my work would be something like that.

This is an old apartment and therefore the mirrors are huge and ornate. They go with the high ornate ceilings. There's one such mirror in the living room and another in the bedroom. Both have intricately-carved borders and a leafy crest on top. In the living room these have been painted over in white, but in the bedroom it's still the original gilt rococo. Both mirrors sit on top of fireplaces and are as big as tombs. I think the descriptive term for them is French regency baroque.

The mirror in the bathroom is pretty big too, and again somewhat ornate. And there are two other mirrors here as well. Not bad for a small, one-bedroom flat.

The problem is I've never been too fond of mirrors. I rarely look into them, and only then to make sure my hair isn't sticking up, or there's no toothpaste showing, or when I'm fine-trimming the beard, to make sure I've missed no section. Oh, there are exceptional other occasions. Once when I got a red eye on a transatlantic flight, for example, I kept checking on the progress of the red's disappearance. Or when I fell on gravel and got an ugly friction-wound on my forehead, I had to first deal with applying the dressing, then keep an eye on how that healing was coming along. Very slowly, as it happened.

As for gazing into the mirror to see if I look okay enough to go out into the world, or – perish the thought – if I look attractive today, the answer is *no way! Que sera, sera*, as the song goes.

Tiny children love the mirror and it's very pleasant to watch them gazing into it. Dogs don't understand it and bark fiercely at the rival dog that's their reflection. I once gave a woman a full-length mirror as a Christmas present. It wasn't ornate or gilded, and it got smashed soon afterwards, and seven years of bad luck followed.

But if I want to look at myself in the mirror regularly or

for lengthy periods, there's plenty opportunity for it in this apartment. I could even stand naked and see everything. And as Monsieur Baudelaire reminds us, according to the immortal principles of 1789, everyone has equal rights; therefore I have the right to behold myself with pleasure or distaste. It is between me and my conscience.

Cher Charles, I have something to tell you, something that might astonish you. I am writing to you almost 150 years after your presence here and there have been some developments you might not have predicted. Some you would have, of course – like rock music, or cinema. Or even LSD, although you probably wouldn't have approved of that (but you'd have liked how The Beatles wrote about it).

Some things never change. Those without money are still here, possibly in greater numbers now. And the floods of displaced creatures from troubled countries are on the increase. This last year has been a shocker. Animals are still becoming extinct too. You'll have known about the poor dodo who'd lived on Mauritius, but he was followed into extinction by the dwarf hippopotamus on nearby Madagascar. The Syrian wild ass is gone too, and the Indian pink-headed duck. And further afield, a celebrated case – the Tasmanian tiger. You'll have heard of this fellow, and will have known he was not a tiger at all, more a wolf with stripes, but he's gone. One will still see him, and probably all the others I've mentioned, taxidermied in museums, but none of them will be moving anymore.

And wars are a must in any period, it seems, but they vary in their approach. The twentieth century brought war to the civilian population, but the twenty-first century has extended this. You may also have predicted aeroplanes, but would you have foreseen two of those planes deliberately crashing into the tallest buildings in New York, and killing thousands? And what about the Nazi gas-chambers that got rid of many more? I've been trying to convey to you in these writings that random killing has come to your beloved Paris, but you would tell me Paris has always had that. It feels different now, though, as if it's bringing in a bad future.

Let me try to stay positive, however. You might not be

surprised to learn that a handful of men have walked on the moon. You liked the moon – you wrote about its benefits. I bet you would have loved to have gone up there with Messrs Armstrong and Aldrin and bounced around a bit, looking back at our blue ball. I hesitate to bring this up, but there are people who want to abandon this planet and colonise the moon. Worse still, they want to emigrate to Mars and live out their last days there. I kid you not. I know it sounds crazy, but these people exist. My belief is they're spawned by the internet. You won't know about that either, and you may or not have expected something like that to emerge, but it contains a few demons – one of your favourite words. What is it, this internet? The dictionary says it's *a global computer network providing a variety of information and communication facilities, consisting of interconnected networks using standardized communication protocols.* Meaningless jargon, I know. Let me start again, then, by telling you a computer is a magic device that is capable of telling you what's going on in the world right now, and giving you private messages too. It also permits snooping and mind-games, and more, but we won't get onto that.

The computer and internet centre in the world is in California, America – in an area called Silicon Valley. The people who work there take it all very seriously. They don't drink wine, Charles, or smoke; they have no interest in good cooking (they stay on strict diets all the time, eating only salads and fruit), they have no fun. What they want is to cease being humans and become robots – the movement is called *Transhumanism.* They want to live forever, to become immortal – and not through poetry. What do you make of that, Charles?

What am I dying to paint, Charles? As I haven't painted anything before I want to be sure, before I start, that my finished work will catch the world's attention – maybe spark a spin-off film that will make me so wealthy I can buy up a vineyard in the Languedoc and learn to make great wine.

I can't decide between two possibilities, so I'll air them both. One concerns a happening after your death, another before your birth. Both bring in your beloved river Seine.

I'll start in the summer of 1905, 6 June, to be very precise. Gabriel Voison successfully flew the first seaplane for 600 metres, at an altitude of 15-20 metres, between the Billancourt and Sèvres bridges. It was a biplane, with an aft tail and a front elevator, supported at rest by two planing floats. My feeling is that this might make a striking painting, if executed correctly, in an old-fashioned way – more Manet, than Paul Klee. I prefer Klee to Manet – in fact, my taste really sits firmly among the abstract terrain, but there would be no possibility of film adaption there.

Let's go back a century earlier, then, to the year 1800. It's still the river Seine, but 120 kilometres north-west of Paris, the city of Rouen. In the early months of that year, a young American inventor called Robert Fulton oversaw the construction of the first submarine in a large workshop in the city. You may well have heard of this, Charles. He called his craft *The Nautilus*. In July he arranged a demonstration on the Seine. A sizeable crowd gathered, among them a small delegation from the new leader, Napoleon Bonaparte. The name that went around the crowd was *un bateau-poisson*.

Fulton climbed from a rowing boat onto the hull of the submarine, carrying a candle. He disappeared through the small hatch, followed by his crew, all carrying candles too. The hatch was closed, and the submarine moved off, heading for a deep spot in the middle of the river.

48

There, suddenly, the grey hulk sank beneath the surface and out of sight. None of the watchers spoke, until after a number of minutes whispers circulated among the crowd. These intensified, and presently a few woman started crying quietly, and one man began praying aloud but was told to shut up. Some people started to leave.

Then, twenty minutes after the dive, a boy shouted and pointed towards the spot where the submarine had gone down. The water was bubbling. There were more shouts, and cheers as the sleek, dripping outline of the conning tower broke the water's surface. A few minutes later the entire craft was afloat. The hatch opened and a smiling Robert Fulton stepped out onto the hull.

On reflection, I'm not so sure that historic little drama would make a painting either. A film yes, but maybe there have been enough U-boat films. Anyway I'm not ready to take up filmmaking. If I were to try a painting, what would I focus on? The submarine going down? The submarine emerging? The inventor standing on the hull smiling? I don't know.

Perhaps you had the right idea, Charles, and I should paint a woman.

19. PARC DES BUTTES CHAUMONT

for Pat Crowley

I had my coffee on the balcony this morning. As I sat there savouring my second cup, I saw a huge crow on a rooftop across the street about five houses down waddle along with a large chunk of a baguette in his beak. He was easily as big as a hen. How had he managed to obtain such a chunk of bread?

I've sometimes felt I was a crow in a previous life. No other bird gives me that feeling – I have a good deal of fondness for the dodo (maybe I pick on that because I have great difficulty imagining myself flying – getting on aeroplanes is hard enough) but I know to imagine myself a reincarnated dodo would be pushing it. I prefer to keep things simple.

It was a summer day in early May, better weather than I'd get in Ireland in August. It was no day to stay in the apartment. I'd go to a park. Paris wasn't as good for green spaces as Berlin, where I'd spent some years, but there were still parks here. I opted for a less obvious one – the *Parc des Buttes Chaumont*. I'd heard of it but had never been there.

I took the Métro to Belleville, reflecting on the fact that the push for the park had come from Napoleon III, late in his regime. Haussmann had chosen the site from unpromising terrain – he was some boy for making over a city, that Haussmann. The Chief Architect of Paris, Gabriel Davioud, had designed it. He liked to create a picturesque, rustic style, apparently, inspired by ancient Rome and by the chalets and bridges of the Swiss Alps. It was opened in 1867, the year of Baudelaire's death, so I doubted if he'd got to see it.

The park was pretty crowded when I got there – lots of families with small children, pairs of young lovers, dogs, but no cats. As I walked in, I saw a diverting if somewhat old-fashioned sight. A young woman in black leggings and top was hoola-hooping or 'hooping', as I believe it's called now, surrounded by a crowd of very young girls, and older boys who were whistling. The twirling red hoop against the black clothing made a pleasing pattern.

It was a hilly park, and reminded me very soon of some of the English parks. The lilac trees were in bloom, spreading purple everywhere. Chestnut trees added their white, and I was fascinated to see a Sophora of Japan pagoda tree, fenced off with a warning sign *Cet arbre remarquable est fragile*. Was that why it was fenced off? Despite the name, I knew it to be a Chinese tree, and that the name 'Sophora' came from two Chinese symbols, one meaning 'wood', one meaning 'demon'. Demon wood, then. I think Monsieur Baudelaire would have approved of this one.

The highlight of the park was the *Temple de la Sibylle* – a miniature version of the famous ancient Roman Temple of Vesta in Tivoli, Italy. This delightful little folly sat atop a partly artificial cliff fifty metres above the rest of the park. Access to it was fenced off, with a note saying it was dangerous to the public, but that didn't stop people climbing over the fence to go up there. I didn't join them but regretted it later. Down below was the artificial lake where ducks swam, none of them with pink heads. To get to this, one traversed a suspension bridge

I bought a mango sorbet, as the day was hot, and thought about the old quarry part of the park was built on, where gypsum and limestone had been mined for the construction of the buildings in Paris. I thought of the past of the other part of the park – the *Gibet de Montfaucon*, where bodies of hanged criminals were displayed from the thirteenth century to 1760, and which after the 1789 revolution became a refuse dump, then a place for cutting up horses and a depository for sewage. I suddenly could smell it all, and hurried out of the park as quick as my legs could carry me. I took refuse in the nearest bar and ordered a carafe of Brouilly.

20. WINDOWS

I'm opening the windows because it's warm. I know Baudelaire said that an open window never reveals as much as one that's closed, but he was helped to arrive at that belief because of the shadowy world of candlelight. There's no candlelight anymore except on the occasion of a power cut, and I don't know if such very mini-disasters ever occur in Paris. We certainly got them all the time in the Donegal I grew up in. A stash of candles was kept where one could easily find it in the dark.

Anyway I don't want my windows revealing anything about me. I don't want some poet across the street, two doors down, seeing me stand at the window, wine glass in hand, daydreaming, and start reconstructing my life story, sprinkling it with tears and a few dollops of blood. Talk about creating a myth! These windows need to be washed, the French windows opening out onto the balcony and Rue Rodier, at least. There must be a tiny window-washing, hovering robot available to hire by the hour these days. I'll pay a visit to the *Bazar de L'Hôtel de Ville*.

I will admit that there are practical problems to keeping the windows open. Those plants all over the balcony must be giving off pollen that might result in hay fever, asthma or worse in the person who inhales it. And there are the loathsome little night visitors who sound like mini Messerschmitts and pierce the exposed skin of an arm with their proboscis to suck your blood that will nourish their babies. I am itchy at the thought of it.

Maybe I will buy a candle this afternoon – a large black candle, and a silver candle-holder with spikes – and tonight I'll put a flame to it, then I'll place it on the table, switch the light off, slip out onto the balcony to sit and look through the glass at it. If I could manage somehow to have me in there with the candle, as well as outside, looking in, I could write a poem about the life I'd imagine for me, the convoluted back-story. Would such writing be classed as autobiography?

52

This morning a huge oil tanker washed up on a beach in Liberia, West Africa, with nobody on board. My guess is that marauding aliens have taken the crew home.

Perhaps it's the constant sight of the pointy white dome of the Basilique du Sacré-Cœur from most bits of Paris I've been to that's got me thinking of spaceships. It was time I paid a visit to Montmartre.

I could have gone straight up Rue Rodier, past Anvers Métro, and on to Montmartre but I opted for a slight detour. I took the tried and trusty Rue des Martyrs right to the top and veered right. The reason was the martyr in the street name. He was a bishop called Saint-Denis who was decapitated on the hilltop of Montmartre in 250 AD. According to the legend he picked up his head and carried it down the hill a bit, before he died, thereby making the whole hill or butte holy.

I stood on the Square Louise Michel in front of the steps leading up to Sacré-Cœur. There were three pointy domes, two of them smaller than the main one. There were two green bronze horseman guarding the basilica. They looked severe. The approach was swarming with people climbing up the steps, or leaning on the low wall in front of the church, or sitting on the grassy slopes. I saw an Indian tour group of twenty or more being led uphill. Suddenly the merry-go-round at the bottom of the steps began to revolve.

I walked on, thinking of the Belle Époque art movement. The artist I'd have most wanted to have met was Modigliani. I'd say we'd have got on. I decided I'd keep going till I got a glimpse of the old windmill, *le Moulin de la Galette*, which Van Gogh painted. I saw it, but looked at the painting online when I got home – it was all brown and dusky blue, with a few dark human figures seen from behind, a higgledy-piggledy lamp atop a perfectly straight post, and a sad French flag on top. I didn't think Paris had brought out the best in Van Gogh.

Le Grand Meneur hardly seemed to come to Paris anymore, since the terror attacks had started. He stayed in his redoubt in the Hautes-Vosges on the slopes of Storkenkopf, although to call his dwelling a redoubt was insulting it. No, it had been erected by the best Alsace builders to have all the grace and impregnability of a small medieval castle. It was so elegantly made that some said the best German builders had been inveigled over the border to assist the French craftsmen.

What was there to bring *le Meneur* Joubert back to polluted and now dangerous Paris? Well, a head of state, even one self-appointed, had occasional matters of state to account for and the parliament was unfortunately still in Paris, a juicy target for any ambitious terrorist, of which there seemed to be a growing number. His fearsome *force de police noire* (well there were some white policemen in that strike force but they were in the minority and could only be part of it if they agreed to go under the black umbrella) did their damnedest to keep the country safe but bombings and shootings still took place. So *le Meneur* got into his bulletproof silver Mercedes very reluctantly, and as seldom as possible, and allowed his psychopath chauffeur Erik to burn up the autoroute to Paris.

There were also the constant visits of foreign heads of state to be dealt with. As much as he could he tried to get these to meet him in his Vosges palace, but many of these dignitaries wanted to see Paris. The city's history and fame were a scourge. And there were the increasingly infrequent performances of his favourite actor, the mime-artist Mathieu Séverin. He was loath to miss any.

What he liked most about Séverin was his outlandish height. The man must be more than two metres tall. The name he got was *La Girafe*. And whether it was because the French word for giraffe was grammatically feminine, he incorporated a female element to his performance – the fluttery eyes, the bum, he did not go so far as to wear fake breasts but his mime made the audience believe he was endowed with the shapeliest of breasts. Whistles were not unknown to greet him on stage.

A shock and a huge disappointment were waiting for *Le Grand Meneur* when Monsieur Yount, much-feared chief of the black police force, came to the Vosges to give a report. He walked into the drawing room, took off his black cap and sat down at the round, walnut table. Basically, he had cracked a lethal terrorist group, he said, and took from his blue leather briefcase a list of names printed out in bold which he slapped on the table just as the coffee was arriving. The top name was Mathieu Séverin, and Yount put his finger on it at once.

Joubert shook his head immediately.

'This cannot possibly be right,' he said. 'Someone must have been telling lies about Mathieu Séverin.'

'*Au contraire, mon Meneur.* He is the ringleader. The brains of the terrorist operation.' Several more stapled pages were placed on the table, and *Le Grand Meneur* snatched these up and read through them rapidly, shaking his head. When he'd finished he laid them face down on the table, sighed loudly and closed his eyes.

'What do you suggest we do?' he asked.

'I can round him and the others up at dawn tomorrow. They can be executed in the evening, or the following morning. Whenever you think best. Or do you think we should turn the execution into a public spectacle, and make an example of the treachery?

'Maybe. Let me think about it.'

Le Meneur remained perturbed long after Yount had departed, but the evidence had seemed irrefutable. He rang for his valet and asked for another coffee, and a glass of cognac. What, or who had taken over Séverin? He had thought of him almost as a friend. Had he not showered favours on him – to be rewarded with this apparent treachery? No, the word 'apparent' had to be sadly deleted. The worst thing was the question of how he was going to do without seeing Séverin ever again.

Then a small voice that rarely ever spoke to him reminded him he was *le Meneur* of France and could do what he wanted, could pardon who he liked. Who gave a damn about how Yount would react to this? He felt so much better he pushed away the glass of cognac unfinished. The valet would enjoy it.

The following afternoon *Le Grand Meneur* got into the back seat of the Mercedes and asked Erik to get him to Paris as quickly as possible. All the other cars on the autoroute bound for the capital were in danger.

At 6 pm they drove up Boulevard Voltaire and soon after, pulled into Rue Nicolas Appert and stopped at the *Comédie Bastille*. The poster on the wall of the theatre advertising tonight's show had been pasted over with the announcement of a replacement show, a rare performance by the great mime-artist Mathieu Séverin. Twice on the way in to Paris, an advertisement for the event had been aired on the radio. And Paris has always been great for word of mouth news of a show spreading quickly.

Le Meneur put on his dark glasses and he and Erik went into the theatre. The latter was carrying a bulky grey canvas bag. They asked to be let go backstage.

At 8 pm they were sitting in the box reserved for important members of the audience. Erik was the only other occupant of the box, the other seats remained empty. An open bottle of a decent Médoc sat on a small table, beside one glass.

A burst of Mozart's jollier music introduced the mime

artist, who sashayed into the spotlight. Immediately one was put in mind of two things – a tall elegant woman, possibly Japanese, who liked to dance, and a giraffe swishing through branches in the evening, the eyes in the high head looking for the choicest leaves. Séverin was really on form tonight. The music had stopped, and the audience was truly being treated to his art of silence. The soul of each person there was being spoken to. The secrets of their lives were being re-opened. The artist grimaced, smiled, spun in a circle, laughed, and cried real tears. He was every beautiful woman who'd existed. He was not just the last giraffe, but all the lovely animals who'd ever become extinct. And when he did his famous party piece – the climbing of the invisible ladder – he went higher up than ever he'd gone before. The audience went wild, *le Meneur* heartily joining in. How Séverin climbed the empty air was a secret he'd never revealed, despite being begged to do so.

He must have been three metres up when the deafeningly loud hissing noise came in stereo from both sides of the theatre, meeting in the ears of the artist. At the same time, two blinding pencil-thin beams of light attacked his eyes. He froze in mid-air, then somersaulted as he fell, landing on his head on the stage. He lay there unmoving.

For a moment absolute silence filled the theatre, then the uproar grew. *Le Grand Meneur* sat through it all, without uttering a sound. He was poleaxed with sadness. He poured a glass of claret and took a deep draught of it. He knew he'd just lost the most supreme artist he'd ever known, and one of his few reasons for living.

23. DAWN

After another night of near sleeplessness I watched the dawn again creep into the room. Well, it felt like I was approaching somewhere, not something coming to me. The painting that jumped strongly into my mind was the Swiss painter Arnold Böcklin's best-known work, the spooky *Totesinsul* (Island of the Dead). In the painting, a boat approaches a desolate and rocky islet with tall cypress trees that are hemmed in by precipitous cliffs that have sepulchral portals and windows cut into them. The boat is manoeuvred by an oarsman sitting in the stern, and standing in the bow is a tall figure dressed completely in white. Behind this figure is what seems to be a coffin. Böcklin painted several versions of this work between 1880 and 1886, and I have seen at least two of them. The artist described it as a dream picture – 'It must produce such a stillness that one would be awed by a knock on the door,' he said. If someone were to knock on my door now, I thought, I'd be more than awed.

I slid out of bed and headed for the kitchen. Are the people one knows and loves ever further from us than at dawn? Is one even properly alive at this hour? To call that grey sky sepulchral, and even more the walls and skylights opposite, where the blinds are never raised, does not seem at all an exaggeration. Baudelaire never wrote about the dawn but he wrote about its opposite, the dusk. It excited the mad, he said. The evening twilight sky brought to his mind a ballerina's attire. The dawn sky suggests to me a hospital gown, if not a shroud.

Perhaps I had landed on the *Totesinsul* without realising it. I shook my head and chose a CD to play – the moustachioed Italian trumpeter, Enrico Rava. If anything could yank me back to the land of the living it was contemporary European jazz, especially if given the Italian jolt. Some of Enrico's trumpet flourishes suggest the movement of a ballerina.

I prime the little espresso machine and set it on the gas flame. I slice an orange into eight sections and suck them dry. Did I always find the dawn this difficult (insomnia is not a new phenomenon in my life)? I can't remember enough dawns to answer that, but two come to mind that seemed nothing but positive – that showed me the world in a new way, one might say. The first was when I was a teenager in Donegal. I couldn't sleep and when dawn lightened the curtains I got up and opened them. I needed to look, as there was a noise that puzzled me. The pebbled yard down below was completely covered in hundreds of gulls and crows, mingling and moving among each other in complete harmony. What I'd heard was nothing less than bird contentment. The second example happened ten or fifteen years later in London. I was living in a flat in Maida Vale that had a back entrance to a private communal park. One night I gave into the temptation and took LSD. The trip I went on was mixed, but not all bad. The best was at the end – as dawn arrived I slipped out the back door into the garden, and there I experienced possibly the most beautiful thing I've ever done – I heard each and every bird's song individually, like stereo multiplied a thousand times. *Cher Charles*, you might have been interested to hear of this.

Yes, I like ports, too. I'm not so keen on airports. Sète is a port I know pretty well. I think of the place as a kind of scruffy Venice, with its canals, and purely French tourists. And its two-tier port. The inner port is crowded with yachts and fishing boats, while the outer is where the big ferryboats come in, or go out from. I've stood with my elbows on the jetty wall, watching one slide out, lights already on, even though it's still bright, and I've imagined I was one of the passengers, heading for a week in Tangiers. Then I've dropped into the port bar for a Ricard. It has never occurred to me to book a passage.

Paul Valéry lies above the port, in *le Cimetière Marin*. He has become his poem. The ferry goes from Sète to Barcelona too. It must have been fun to have travelled there on an old, rigged sailing ship – the walk up the Ramblas to eat shellfish and get drunk in the *Mercat de Boqueria* would have felt earned. Coming back to Sète, though, I'm wondering if U-boats ever docked at the port in the 1940s.

The biggest port I've been in is the Port of Hamburg. Curiously, it isn't on the sea at all, but on the river Elbe. This does not deter cruise liners from coming in to take passengers across the Atlantic, or on a journey up the Baltic, with many stops along the way. Most of the active U-boats set out from the Port of Hamburg to terrorise the Atlantic shipping during the war. The first time I visited the port I inquired in a bar if there were any old rusting U-boats that could be bought cheaply. Great mirth ensued and I was bought a beer.

A niece of mine, after too much beer, fell into the water between a fishing boat and the quay in Greencastle Port, in my native Donegal. Fortunately, someone dived in and rescued her. Not far away is Inishtrahull Island where U-boats used to dock during the First World War to barter whisky for food. There's a lovely little port there, going completely to waste. Another Donegal island, further south, is Aranmore – a zany place, where old cars are left abandoned in fields, priests are run off the island, and the pubs stay open all night, or until the bar runs dry. I was once waiting at the port there to return to the mainland – I was the last car, just about to drive on, when a hearse arrived at considerable speed, horn blaring, and nipped onto the boat in front of me. I had to wait hours for the next ferry.

It used to be once a year, now it's every five years. Bad luck on the babies born in the wrong years, but cuts are everywhere, and caprice is always a player when it comes to largesse being doled out. Not to mention the element of the arbitrary, the subjective taste of the donor, and the role of Mr Luck himself. And, as far as I know, no other country apart from France still hosts such a gathering of the Fairies to bestow their gifts on the chosen and highly fortunate newborn. Russia was the last previous country, but the cold, brutally rational years that followed their particular revolution put paid to the Fairies. One might imagine that Ireland should have some ceremony like this but the perception there is that Fairies have never brought a single person any good.

Anyway, I arrived at the Boulevard des Capucines and made my way to the Palais Garnier, thinking the Fairies must have some clout to have swung such a venue for their gathering. Approaching the awesome building I asked what the hell had been wrong with Le Corbusier to have dismissed it as a lying art, a décor of the grave. I don't have much problem with the lying part, as I believe (I've made this clear before) that all art has to lie its way to the truth, but décor of the grave? Really? I'd never seen a grave that approached this grandeur, not even the most elaborate tomb.

I made for the Grand Escalier, walking past the enigmatic stone female figures holding torches. The high vault was pretty impressive, with its marble of various colours. I went exploring where I wasn't supposed to, but I had to find the Chagall ceiling that had been unveiled in 1964. It was more than worth tracking down with all its blue, red and green, and its female figures, mainly if not all undressed, that were probably meant to denote dancers but could be fairies. I retraced my steps to the path I was meant to be taking, thinking these Fairies had picked the perfect spot.

Eventually I found the Salon du Glacier where the ceremony was taking place. It was a bright rotunda with a circular ceiling painted by Clairin which showed what might be fairies dancing around in a mist. And dangling down from the middle of the ceiling was a sumptuous chandelier. Perfect, then. I went in search of a drink. A tapestry on the wall showing a Chinese lady pouring tea made me nervous – would only tea be served? I was presented at the drinks table with a glass of perfectly good Médoc, though, and I took it away to survey the room, but not before acknowledging that the salon evoked the aesthetic of the Belle Époque.

It was quite full, but not thronged, to my surprise. I'd anticipated all the newborn babies in France, not just in Paris, being brought here in the hope of being set up for life. Maybe most parents no longer believed in fairies or unearned largesse. There were still more babies here than ever I'd seen in a room together – they lay in little red cots all over the round room, with their parents in attendance, and paths for the Fairies to stroll past them. They were noisy, as would have been expected, but above their bawling, a beautifully moody piece of classical music could be heard, and it took me a while to recognise it was Rachmaninov's composition, *Isle of the Dead*, written after he'd seen – in Paris in 1907 – a black and white reproduction of the Böcklin painting of that name. That was a good joke as a piece of music to be played at a gathering of the newborn.

It's time I started talking about the Fairies. First, though, I'll explain why there were no television cameras or photographers in evidence. Apparently, the Queen of the Fairies, Tiphaine, had made a condition that if the event were continuing, there must be no publicity whatsoever. She couldn't prevent the police being present, given the

63

current terrorist threat, but as taking photographs with mobile phones was also forbidden, the police could ensure that ban would hold.

Tiphaine was a scary-looking lady – tall, heavily made-up eyes, and spiky jet-black hair that showed she'd approved of the punk movement. It was impossible to say what age she was representing, although I knew Fairies were ageless. They were still supposed to select an age to pretend to be while they were here. The other Fairies present – there looked to be about thirty of them, all female (were there no male Fairies anymore?) had chosen a variety of ages.

It was quickly clear that each of the Fairies could choose one baby only. I got another glass of wine and started following one – an apparently very old woman with long white hair, wearing a flowing white skirt – who had yet to make her choice. I wanted to see what grounds she'd have for choosing. When the favour came it seemed to be completely arbitrary. Oh, her eyes kept closing after she'd stood in front of each baby, then opening again as she'd moved slowly on. With the lucky child, however, she seemed to float a half-metre from the ground, and was that a lime green aura emanating from her? Her ancient face became lit up and radiant, and yes, beautiful, as she gazed at the baby's face. The child was a boy, called Tristan – the Fairy declared he would become a major golfer. It was time France had one of those, I thought to myself.

There was one startling incident that caused a bit of a stir, and had a pair of policemen escorting a Fairy out of the room, while the particular baby associated with that Fairy plus his parents were escorted out by two more policemen. I needed to ask a few strangers what was going on and discovered that the baby had been told he would become a very famous terrorist.

The ceremony ended with all the Fairies bar one (how could the police keep a Fairy in captivity?) standing in a line on the stage, with the chosen babies lying at their feet. None of these little people were crying now, as if they somehow were aware of their good fortune. It was announced that the ratio of girls to boys chosen was two to one. That sounded like bias to me.

At any rate, the Fairies sang some kind of between-worlds song, at the end of which one disappointed father who'd imbibed a bit much came up to the foot of the stage to remonstrate because his baby had not been chosen. The Fairies chorally hissed at him so loudly that he fell down holding his ears. Then one by one, led by their Queen, they filed through the crowd to the foyer, where they opened a window and flew in formation down the Avenue de L'Opéra. I looked out after them and saw that they were joined by the arrested Fairy somewhere above the Louvre.

26. LES SALTIMBANQUES

I was walking from the Louvre to Place St-Michel along the Seine when I noticed a crowd gathered under a large linden tree. As I approached, I thought how much I'd liked to walk down Unter den Linden when I'd lived in Berlin, and now I saw again how attractive the light green seeds of the linden tree were against the darker green of the leaves. I was also agog to see what had caused the crowd to gather.

As I neared, I heard a mother say to her little boy *'Regardez, Sébastien, les saltimbanques'.*

Saltimbanques? This was a new word to me. I had a quick look on my iPhone and came up with the translation 'mountebank'. I pushed my way as politely as possible through the crowd until I had a good view. It was a family of street performers. They had improvised a small stage on the wide pavement, and a father, mother and ten-year-old or so boy were up there. The man was dressed in a striking yellow and blue outfit with white leggings and black shoes, and was banging a little drum rhythmically while the boy in a checked black and white jumpsuit capered about, playing thumb rolls on a tambourine, with a black and white dog dancing in perfect step alongside him. The woman, dressed all in white, sat on a stool playing quick dance music on a red tin whistle. On her head was a white floppy hat, sitting on which was a snowy owl who periodically flew in a circle over the heads of the crowd, coming back to land on the white hat. It was a scene worthy of being painted by the young Picasso, or the old Chagall. Or maybe by Gustav Doré. The boy on stage didn't look in the best of health, but I hoped I was wrong. The effect of the whole performance was strange and utterly charming. And the little troupe seemed to have emerged from another era – from that of Baudelaire, even.

I was puzzled by the translation offered by my iPhone, however. What I understood by the English word 'mountebank' (which seemed very archaic) was either a person who sold quack medicines in public places, or a charlatan. These performers were no fakes. And yet, the English word, like the French, seemed to suggest the jumping up onto a stage. I'd have to revisit my Shakespeare plays – I seemed to remember that he'd liked using that word.

When the white hat came round I put a 20 euro note into it, took a quick photograph of *les saltimbanques* and made my way to the nearest Métro. I was almost surprised to see cars and motorbikes clogging the road.

I'd never been in Paris for Bastille Day. I'd been here in July but for some reason never on the fourteenth. I'd been in Sète on that date but not a lot ever happened down there. Not a lot would happen for me here today.

I went out for lunch and had a bowl of *soupe à l'oignon* with a glass of red wine. I headed back to the apartment. Whatever official celebrations were planned for tonight, the private ones where the French let their hair down and got pissed wouldn't be written about on the Internet. Were there any surprises to be expected? Small planes flying above the city pulling the lines of one of Baudelaire's most famous Paris poems? That old favourite, Eric Cantona, kicking a football from the roof of the Louvre into the Seine, and reading into the microphone a gnomic haiku he'd written about the act in advance of the event? And was it permissible for foreigners resident in Paris to join in the celebrations?

I had no option other than head out into the city and take what would confront me. First, though, I thought it expedient to ring a French friend and arrange to meet up. This duly happened, on condition that we went to a very old brasserie near Les Halles and ate nineteenth-century French food, washed down with a decent Bordeaux. I had *rognons de veau aux échalotes* to satisfy him, and I didn't let on I was more than happy to eat that dish, or that my grandfather used to make it.

We didn't overdo it, and shortly after midnight I headed back to the Rue des Martyrs district. I was soon back at one of my local stations, Notre-Dame-de-Lorette. The train had been full of unusually friendly Parisians, most of whom were at least tipsy. As I emerged from the metro, into Rue St-Lazare I was astonished to be approached by a burly man in a Stetson hat and an expensive, dark green suit, with a tiger cub on a leash. He eyeballed me, seeing straight away

I was a foreigner.

'Would you do me the courtesy, young man, of joining me in my hotel for a drink?'

I could tell from the accent he was Texan, and I was at least as old as he was, but I wasn't averse to a further drink. Besides, I was curious about the tiger. One didn't see them often in Paris.

We went to his hotel – a chic, small one called Hôtel Brittany which was very close by. There was a tiny hotel bar which I was led to, and without my being asked what I wanted, two large glasses of Jack Daniels were set in front of us. The tiger lay on the carpet staring at me, and this made me slightly nervous. I knew that tigers and other big cats could be legally kept as pets in Texas, but how in hell had he got her into France? There must be real oil money here, I thought.

'You must be asking what takes a Texan to Paris for Bastille Day?' the man asked, then answered himself.

'I have French blood. The name is Théron. A forebear of mine was big in the American civil war so I have a soft spot for the French Revolution. I come every year.'

'I see', I said. I omitted to tell him I too had French blood. In truth, the whiskey on top of the wine was beginning to get to me. I threw back a large glass of water, and glanced at the tiger. As if just a look was enough provocation, the cub got to her feet and started shaking her bum, an action I knew from domestic cats meant she was getting into attack mode. I looked at Mr Théron, who began to laugh. He got up from his bar stool and walked towards the tiger cub who charged at him – and jumped up to put her paws on his shoulder and lick his face. I shook my head, as the Texan laughed even more loudly.

'See how lovely my little lady is?'

He kissed her, then picked up his whiskey glass, which

he swigged from, then put it to the tiger's lips and angled it forward, so a good dollop of whisky went into the feline mouth.

'We all get to be happy on Bastille Day', he said.

He was busy cuddling his tiger when I slipped away. I had no need of further whiskey and I was disgusted at his idiotic dosing of his pet with the stuff. There was surely more of that to follow before the night was out. The act seemed to me to epitomise what it meant to be American, or at least Texan. I hoped his tiger ate him.

There are worse things to do on a bright, dry day than go on a literary walk in the *Quartier Latin*, led by a tall Belgian novelist of Russian extraction. We met at a stylish bookshop called *Arbre à Lettres*, a name that appealed to me as I liked the idea of a tree of letters, not so much as a metaphor for a poem, but for the writer's developing *œuvre*. On second thoughts, I rejected it as being a bit grand.

The novelist's name was Eugène Savitzkaya and he was writer-in-residence at the bookshop. I did like the idea of going on the walk with him. He was living the life of a *flâneur* in Baudiere's meaning of the world, walking though bits of Paris, writing about them. Wasn't that exactly what I was trying to do?

He held up the wishbone of a magpie in place of the umbrella the normal tour guides brandish, and we followed him up Rue Mouffetard, a group of about fifteen or so, most of them French. Every now and then we'd stop at a house, and the novelist would tell us stuff about it. He would also sometimes scribble in a notebook. I strained to catch some of the meaning of what he was saying to us. I gradually gathered (or thought I did) that he had invented a nineteenth-century poet – an impoverished, fairly unsuccessful fellow he gave the name of Hegésippe Moreaux to. The next house he stopped at was that of a real poet of the time for whom everything seemed to have been going fine, although which of us has heard of him now? We were told the successful poets were part of a confraternity called *Les Fées Libres* and these were allowed to suck the milk of poetry directly from the breasts of the Muses. Yeah! And Baudelaire was the king of those free fairies, or would have been if the confraternity had existed. Monsieur Savitzkaya was full of fanciful stories. It did offer a contrast to poor Moreaux, though.

We stopped at a building with a plaque stating that

René Descartes had lived there. For some reason it was here that the Belgian pulled out a medieval bestiary and read a passage about the medical importance of beavers as was believed at the time. Apparently there was a gland in the beaver's testicle that cured practically everything. Even the beavers knew this, we were told, so if one was pursued by a hunter he bit his own testicles off and threw them at the man with the musket.

We veered off Rue Mouffetard, pausing for a while at a house where a poet and philosopher called Benjamin Fondane lived until he was taken away to Auschwitz in 1944. Earlier times of terror in Paris. Fondane, I learned, wrote about Rimbaud and possibly Baudelaire. I made a note I should read up about him. Someone in the group then informed me that Hemingway and Joyce had also lived in this area, with plaques to prove it, but we were not brought to see these. Instead, we climbed down some steps to what used to be a Roman arena, and is still called *Arènes de Lutèce*.

It was still big and circular and sandy underfoot, but believe it or not, it went lost for a time. It took the actions of a preservation committee that included Victor Hugo to draw attention to the buried archaeological treasure, until eventually the arena was restored and established as a public space.

And a public space was very definitely what it was now. There were three games of *boules* in progress, and two gangs of boys were kicking footballs around. Scores of other people were strolling about and the seats held groups of old men watching everything. It was into this setting that Eugène Savitzkaya had brought us, and he immediately announced he was going to stand on his head.

That was a good joke, I thought, but then I saw him remove his shoes and socks, and take out of a big, blue bag a pair of heavy worsted trousers, and a large jacket of the same course material. He proceeded to put these on over his existing clothes and told us that this was the garb he imagined Hegésippe Moreaux wearing. Next out of the bag came four sturdy wooden blocks, two of them with a green cushion affixed. He put two blocks on top of each other, about fifteen centimetres apart. On went a black woollen hat and upside down he went, his shoulders on the green cushions. His bare feet stuck into the air. His head was about five centimetres from the ground so strictly speaking he wasn't standing on his head, but that was quibbling.

The head at the bottom started speaking in a poetic sounding monologue. I didn't pick up much of this, I'm afraid. Someday I'd take steps to improve my French. A few boys who were fooling around on the level above, behind a low wall, stopped and took an interest in the strange upended man. Three policemen came to investigate, wondering, I imagine, if this was an unusual form of terrorism, but soon turned and walked away. A man smoking a pipe came to take a dekko. Loads of other people drifted over to look on. The monologue continued, and I saw pages being turned underneath the head.

I took to trying to visualise this arena in Roman times. I'd spent my twenty-first birthday in the south of France, picking grapes, and as a birthday treat I'd been brought to a bullfight in the old Roman arena in Nîmes. In Roman times when the gladiators came here to fight each other, 15,000 people would have been seated around, watching. I suddenly wanted to bring here the Texan tiger cub I'd met and set her against a few poets I knew. I knew people who'd pay a lot to see that.

The *boules* games went on, oblivious to the great act that was being performed. The footballs kept being banged by the boys, the burliest of which was wearing a Paris

St-Germain jersey, with the name Ibramovich on the rear-side. Suddenly, Savitzkaya fell on his back with a muffled crash, and lay there, arms out, legs slightly spread, head twisted a bit to the left. And from a cassette player laid on the ground another monologue boomed out. It had a refrain which I got: *je ne suis pas fatigué* – and this statement seemed to be applied to all parts of the speaker's body, but the man lying on the sand looked exhausted in every way.

The performance ended soon after to a spattering of keen applause. The novelist did not bow, but as he removed the heavy clothes he leaned down to pick something up from the ground. It was a cat's eye, he announced, and held up a red marble, showed it all round, like a priest does with the host at the communion of the mass, then slipped it into his pocket, and smiled broadly.

I went into *Les Fossoyeurs* and collapsed in a seat, brushing the rain from my coat. What a creepy name for a bar, I thought, even though we were right by the back entrance of Père Lachaise.

There was a pub in Dublin very close to Glasnevin Cemetery whose unofficial name was *The Gravediggers*. I can't remember the real name of the pub, as it was never used by anyone who drank there. In this Parisian bar the word was the official name.

Creepy or not, I had to say I found the name greatly amusing, also thirst-inducing. I began to feel I was in a sixteenth-century Dutch painting, shown drinking wine and eating a sausage, while a human skull stared at me from the table. I went to the bar and ordered a carafe of red *vin du moment*, then sat there, sipping the wine, trying to speculate on how I might die. Would it be in Paris in the rain? Would a suicide bomber reduce me to bloody pieces, or a cold shooter empty ten bullets into me?

I put a stop to that kind of thinking in a rather oblique way – I thought of the last grave I'd visited, that of Mr Beckett. Coincidentally, I'd seen a strange, short video on YouTube a few days previously, featuring the small cottage Beckett had built in Issy-sur-Marne with the money he'd earned from *Waiting for Godot*. It wasn't anything much to look at, the little house, but apparently he used to like to spend time there, away from the stresses of his life in Paris. In the video his old neighbour was talking about this. She recounted how Beckett had loved mowing the lawn, and how he'd had great problems with moles. The molehills kept erupting all over the lawn, and Beckett had to flatten them all, and kill any mole he encountered. The woman said there were no moles now.

As I finished my wine I could see some of the tombs through the gates of the cemetery. If I'd indulged in cigars,

I would have smoked one now. I decided I felt in the mood to pay a visit to the cemetery. I settled up my bill and headed out.

The rain had stopped and the sun was shining so much the crown of my head quickly felt warm. The flowers must have been enjoying it. Insects were buzzing and flitting about, lit up by the sunbeams. The traffic noise from beyond the walls was still audible, but muted. I wandered aimlessly down a tree-lined, winding path, wondering at the huge population of the land of the dead. Undone, undone, all their hopes and dreams. Yeah. That boat was pulled up on the islet's shore and the cypresses were glowering.

I came to a tomb of some unknown family. It was the shape and size of a telephone box, those old obsolete things that used to stand on the street before the ascent of the mobile phone, or *portable*, as the French called it. I stepped inside and knelt down, but instead of praying, I thought of an old man, long dead, whom I knew when I'd first lived in London. He'd grown up in a wealthy family in Highgate, and his family (as was not uncommon among the well-off) had a large tomb in Highgate Cemetery. Because the Victorian English had a paranoia of being interred while still alive, the tomb had a phone inside which was connected to a phone in the family house. If someone woke up in there then, they could simply call and asked to be let out. Simple and sensible, I thought.

I left the tomb and carried on. I should really visit a few famous dead people, as I was in here. I'd give Jim Morrison a miss, but why not pay a quiet homage to Oscar Wilde? I'd once had to read some of his fairy stories as part of a children's festival in the Barbican, and I'd found them terrific, and quite dark. And after that I'd visit the tomb of Molière. I'd seen one of his plays, *Le Misanthrope*, in Annaghmakerrig, County Monaghan – it had been in

French and I'd been extremely surprised how much I'd got out of it, despite my limited command of the language.

Suddenly I felt this strong urge to revisit the tomb I'd just vacated. It was as if someone were commanding me to do so. I retraced my steps, walked in and knelt down again. Then a French voice spoke in my head, and weirdly was immediately translated into English – I could hear the French words slightly before the English. I was being extremely disrespectful of the dead, I was told. I was showing them no regard at all. A cemetery, no matter how famous, was not a tourist high-point. The only graves or tombs I should allow myself to visit were the resting places of family or close friends. The dead need and deserve their privacy too. And as for the ridiculous competitiveness that was more and more prevalent in life – among politicians, business people, and yes, among writers and artists too – you living people should know that the only prize worth winning was death, everything else is a frippery. You'll find this out soon enough. In the meantime you should conserve your energy, and desist from disturbing the sleep of those of us who've won the prize. With that the voice stopped, and I was almost pushed out of the tomb.

My mind was reeling. I had no option but to return to *Les Fossoyeurs* and have another carafe of the red wine. And another.

The Quai de Bourbon on the Île St-Louis was unusually crowded as I walked down it, looking for a famous ice-cream place I remembered being brought to one previous time I was in Paris. Trouble was I couldn't remember the name. I walked as briskly as the hordes would allow me, keeping an eye out for pictures of ice-cream cones. Suddenly a man brushed against me in passing and I somehow knew strongly I'd wanted all my life to meet this special personage. The smile and the wink he gave me persuaded me he too was not averse to a meeting. I could not resist returning both the smile and the wink, although I never indulge in winking, believing it to be too arch.

I turned and looked for him. He was easy enough to spot, being resplendent in a dark red suit that looked like it had been designed by Armani. His hair was black and long, and beautifully styled. His face brought to mind medieval Italian depictions of the visages of angels.

He did not turn to greet me, but he knew I was there. I stuck close to him and began following down some hidden steps to an underground club of some kind. The door opened by itself to moody jazz music that was extremely tasteful and not too loud. The place was crowded but none of the men and woman there, though all unusually beautiful, looked happy. I'd never seen eyes that looked so empty, or faces that showed how much they wanted to feel more alive. There was no dancing, or kissing, or even much walking around. No one seemed to be drunk, either.

By the time I sat down at a table with my new friend I felt I'd known him for fifty years. We ate exquisite *foie gras* with mustard seeds and green onion, drenched in *jus d'oie*. We drank an inordinate quantity of the best St-Émilion I'd ever put down my gullet, and weirdly, after some hours, I realised I was no more drunk than he was. The wine kept coming.

Then a delectable young woman who looked like she wanted to hang herself or had hanged herself brought along a pack of playing cards – an amazing-looking deck that had a different imaginary animal painted on the back of each card. My companion favoured a variant of poker called Texas Hold 'Em, one that I knew was preferred by the professionals. He played so well he might have been a professional himself. I fancied myself as a poker player, so I foolishly pitted myself against him, despite the high stakes he insisted we play for. And so I lost my soul to him. I wasn't too bothered, I confessed, as I didn't believe in the concept of a soul, or an afterlife, even, though who then were these people in the club with me? At any rate I displayed an admirable indifference to the loss.

We tired of the card-game soon afterwards and took to chatting in earnest. We discussed America and Russia, and the pros and cons of the Internet. We debated the current state of international football, of which my companion had a low view. We got onto the arts, which again he felt was not as fully-firing as in previous eras. What later poet, he asked, had improved on Baudelaire? I had to agree with him on that one. He wanted to know why no-one on earth realised how absurd they were being in their beliefs and outrageous demands. His own worldwide bad name didn't seem to bother him too much, but he assured me that what he most wanted to do was abolish superstition. He confided that only once had he been apprehensive of his own powers, and that had been when he'd heard a clever Australian priest (and he listened to them all) declaim from the pulpit that the Devil's most skilful trick was to convince you he doesn't exist.

I wanted to ask him about his old friend and sparring-partner, God, but as I'd convinced myself I no longer believed in Him, I didn't. I doubted The Shining One had ever granted such a lengthy audience to any mortal. I didn't want to overstep my welcome. In the end, as the first streaks of dawn lightened the windows, the great personage fêted by so many poets over the centuries, said to me: 'I'd like you to keep a happy memory of me, so to compensate for the inestimable loss of your soul I'm giving you the stake you'd have won if you'd been luckier. All your desires from now on will be realised for you. You'll be immensely powerful, you'll be adored, rich, you'll flit from country to country at will. All the loveliest women in the world will fall for you.'

If it hadn't been for the crowd of people around me I'd have thrown myself on the ground in front of this generous being and kissed his green crocodile-skin shoes, thanking him for his immense kindness. But very quickly after I had finally taken my leave, I began to have serious doubts about his delivering his promises to me. If I'd believed in God I might have prayed to Him right then to ask him to make sure the Devil kept his word.

I didn't know how much asparagus was eaten in Paris around Baudelaire's time but he'd have loved the odour it gives to a person's urine. One could call it a kind of dour perfume, only sniffable in the small private room that's the toilet. Anyway, the real question I wanted to ask Monsieur Baudelaire was, if among the *saltimbanques* he witnessed in Paris, there was ever a snake-charmer. Just yesterday I asked someone if there were snakes in France, and the answer I got (if one could call it that) was inconclusive.

The more I thought of it, the more convinced I was that Baudelaire had certainly seen at least one snake-charmer. In fact, he must have sought out many. It was clear from his writings that he was fascinated by the Devil, and if ever there was a creature that seemed to have been created by that sinister fellow, it was a snake. And there were many varieties of snake.

In several parts of the world there were delicacies of snake cooked in one way or another. I knew snake soup was popular in Hong Kong. I may even have seen that on a menu in Shanghai but I foolishly passed. An advice that was once given to me by a foodie was that one should never hesitate to eat what's beyond one's safety zone.

I once saw a television film set in a dinner party of bored gourmets – the dish of the evening was clearly roast human leg, and even this palled for the most jaundiced of the gathered chompers.

'I've eaten everything that can be eaten', he said.

'No, you haven't', said his companion. 'You still have to experience the delectability of eating a human ghost.'

So off they went to the sacristy of an ancient church where a hundred years previously a priest had been murdered. Armed with butterfly net, small frying pan and gas burner they waited, and ate.

This had been written by Kazuo Ishiguro, and not by

Baudelaire, but the latter had clearly been an influence. The quick-fried ghost looked to have the consistency of squid, which must be similar in texture to snake.

One is advised to beware of rattlesnakes, as they can still bite after they're dead. Apart from that, the preferred approach (although they can be eaten raw, apparently) is to behead a snake, bury it, then skin and clean it, then pierce chunks with a wooden skewer and grill over the coals. It sounds delectable. I'd eat it tomorrow, with a decent wine.

The most stylish way to eat a snake, however, would be to charm it first, make it sway and dance to Arab jazz (Anouar Brahem would be good), then swipe its head off with a machete, and get to work in the kitchen and the garden. And maybe, just maybe, it would go with asparagus.

I was beginning to have second thoughts about my idea of branching out into painting. Oh, I could draw a line with graphite as good as any non-professional, but being realistic, a lot more was needed. And painters tended to start scarily young, didn't they? I'd once had the pleasure of visiting the Picasso Museum in Malaga, the city where Pablo grew up. They had some canvases painted by him as a child and they were amazingly accomplished. The museum also had quotes from Picasso, recorded at different stages in his life. One of them was this: 'When I was a child I painted like an adult, now that I'm an adult I keep trying to paint like a child.' Very neat, I'd thought then and still do. I suspected I was incapable of painting like a child or like an adult.

The idea of becoming a forger had forced its inglorious way into my mind, then. I'd tried to bar its entry but couldn't. The outrageous question as to whether Baudelaire had ever done art forgeries or not was even forming in there. I knew he'd been more famous in his lifetime as an art critic than as a poet, and a lot of his friends were artists. Maybe some evening, over wine, Edouard Manet had egged him on to copy a work of his beloved Delacroix, to great hilarity in both men – Manet stepping in occasionally to show what to do. Baudelaire certainly left enough evidence to prove he understood how a painting worked or didn't work. In a famous essay, he recounts joining 'a crowd of fools' standing in front of a canvas, where flies could be seen buzzing about, and Baudelaire was interested in it only because of 'the attraction of the horrible'. He wanted, he writes, '… to study the moral character of a man who had begotten such a piece of criminal extravagance. I wagered that he must be fundamentally evil. I made inquiries and my intuition was gratified to win this psychological wager. I learnt that this monster regularly got up before dawn;

that he had ruined his housekeeper and that he only drank milk.'

Right, that was that, then. I got the feeling that even if the man described had better sleeping patterns and drank good wine he wouldn't have been a better painter. What would Baudelaire have made of the moral character of a forger? Not much, probably. Maybe I should crumple this idea of a new career and drop it in the *poubelle*.

First, though, I'd check out a famous forger of about my own age – a German-born man originally named Wolfgang Fischer who has long operated as Wolfgang Belracchi (taking the surname from his wife, Helene). This duplicitous fellow forged, according to international police, more than fifty works of art, and passed them off successfully, amassing millions of euros. Among the works forged were three by Heinrich Campendonk and five by Max Ernst – his forgery of the latter's painting 'La Fôret' was so good that it fooled Ernst's widow. Belracchi has said he got a special kick out of standing in front of a painting in a big gallery like MOMA, knowing he'd painted it. Well, the police caught up with him and chucked him into a German prison for six years, ordering him to make huge reparations. He got out after three years, however, on condition he only painted in his own name from now on. The interesting thing is that his own paintings now sell for millions anyway, and he goes around New York with the aura of a hippy rock star, while his New York gallerist calls him the Robin Hood of Art.

Not a bad recommendation for the career of a forger, then. I'd give it some serious thought, despite any possible misgivings Baudelaire might have had. The one thing that worried me, though, was that even Belracchi had started young – he'd successfully copied a Picasso painting when he was fourteen.

Was it Pascal who said 'Almost all our misery has come from not being able to remain alone in our rooms'? Baudelaire thought it might have been, but was not sure. And let's take a look at that 'almost' which I'm very glad is there. I can think of lots of misery that had nothing to do with my not having been alone in my room. When I get a rejection email on a train for a piece of work I had high hopes for is one example. Or to go way back, when I returned home to find my white mouse dead when I was eleven or twelve. Or to take a mundane example, when a plane I'm booked on is twelve hours delayed, while I hang about the airport.

I have never had a huge problem with solitude, it is true. As a child I read voraciously, and would find some hidden corner to lurk with my book. The game of golf is one where one can enjoy being alone, especially very early on a beautiful morning. The time when I most felt alone was when the missionaries came to my school and we all had to endure a silent retreat for three days. At the end of that time I felt like one of those astronauts in films who have to stay on the moon for months.

Baudelaire claimed his friend the Devil loved bleak, solitary places where the spirit of murder and lust was more likely to ignite. He decided that this was not really a danger for most of us, though, only for those idle, fanciful folk prone to enigmas and dreaming. The type of person who should most avoid being alone is a chatterbox or maybe a television pundit. But what's to stop these people being verbose in their own company? Did Crusoe, for example, stay quiet on his island before Friday came? According to Elizabeth Bishop in her great poem, 'Crusoe in England', he did not.

And in order to write that poem, Ms Bishop needed to be alone. This did not stop her cooking meals and inviting friends to help her eat the food, and drink wine with her. After this, probably the next morning, she went back to the poem and her solitude.

I feel the French maybe exaggerate the benefits of being alone. That philosopher and writer, Jean Paul Sartre for example, his play *Huis-clos* with its famous line *'L'enfer, c'est les autres.'* Yes, we all know how annoying other people often are, and how strong the urge to escape from them can be. But the two characters Vladimir and Estragon in Beckett's *Waiting for Godot* show that even in an absurdist setting companionship has its importance. It's said Beckett got his inspiration for this play from one or other of two versions of Caspar David Friedrich's painting 'Two Men Contemplating the Moon' which he saw on a trip to Germany in 1936 or '37. In both versions of the painting, one of the men has his hand on the other man's shoulder, a sign of companionship if ever there was one.

Baudelaire quotes the French philosopher and moralist, Jean de la Bruyère (or Delabruyère, as the man signed himself), 'What a great misfortune we cannot be alone', as if to chastise anyone who wants to plunge into a crowd, or go into a busy bar. What about the great French word *fraternité*, the third of the three words that were the rallying cry of the Revolution? I want to close this by giving another quote from de la Bruyère: 'Out of difficulties grow miracles.' I prefer this one. Anyone in an awkward social situation should dwell on that.

I had to push my way onto the Métro yesterday at Franklyn D Roosevelt because it was so crowded. A big, disreputable fellow with long, stringy hair and dirty clothes made it hard for me to get on, as he stood there in the entrance with a shopping trolley, packed with paper and books. I squeezed into a negotiated niche behind him and glowered. He paid no attention, engrossed as he was in reading the book that he had open on top of the pile. It took me two stops to realise what he was reading so intently – a French translation of the Koran!

I was off that Métro train as quick as a rat leaving a corpse the police were arriving at. As I stood there on the platform at Pyramides I began to feel I might have overreacted. The next train rattled and bustled to a halt. This one was quite a bit emptier. I even found a seat. I was busy making notes on an envelope when I had an interruption – I was about five stops from Cadet where I was intending to get off. It was a busker, of a sort – I was used to them from the U-Bahn in Berlin. There, they would usually be Romanian gypsies playing the violin off-key and singing maudlin, clichéd songs, but this was different. For a start, a CD machine was switched on and rap music was issuing. Then the young man began singing something in Arabic that kept to the insistent rhythm. He didn't look Arabic any more than the man on the first train with the Koran had, but still. I didn't get off this train prematurely, but I was glad when my stop came.

I came up the stairs at Cadet and there was a child beggar sitting on the top step, holding out a plastic cup. He was barely eight years old. He had black hair, which was covered with a black hood. He had an Arab complexion.

Shaking my head, I took the lift up to my flat. I had no food in, I quickly realised, and I was hungry, so I had to go out again. I had no desire to go far. There was an Algerian restaurant up the street, I remembered. I'd been wanting to try it out for while.

I walked in and it was completely empty. Nevertheless, a very polite waiter came out to me and sat me down at a window table. I ordered couscous with lamb and a carafe of Algerian wine. While I waited I began to admire the table lamp. It was a metal camel with the lamp-pole sticking out of its back. Around the bulb was a fringe of tiny red beads strung on white string, and depicted on the fringe, three times, was a basic portrayal of a woman in red, blue and black.

The couscous was fine, the Algerian wine also. The emptiness of the restaurant was pretty spooky, though, especially when I remembered what had been happening in Paris recently, and the fears that were abroad – the soldiers with machine guns that were walking around the local streets. Restaurants like this were clearly being blanked now, a reaction to the not too-distant shootings and bombs. When I descended the stairs to the basement toilet, and found the stair-carpet very worn, I knew there had been a decent and regular clientele here before. This drop in popularity was a very unfair development, I felt. The standard of the cooking was still good. Nobody should be held to blame for terrorism because of their skin colour, or their arbitrarily presumed connection to the perpetrators.

The motorbikes parked on the street outside with blue hoods on looked like dogs waiting to be set loose on walkers by. This was the thought that went down the street with me to Cadet Métro. I was on my way to meet an old friend from Donegal who happened to be staying for a few weeks in Paris, in the Irish College in the Latin Quarter. He was a sculptor and was spending a lot of time in the Picasso Museum in the Marais.

We had agreed to meet for a drink in the Canal St-Martin district which was a short walk from the museum. He'd opted for a famous old watering hole called *Chez Prune*, which was right on the canal on Quai de Valmy. I liked the name, as whatever it meant in French, when I'd been at boarding school in Ireland in the late '60s, a common insult we received was 'You prune, you'. I still feel like a prune from time to time. Anyway, it was good to see him again, and it felt kind of special to meet him abroad, especially in such a salubrious part of a special city. We embraced and found a table inside, then ordered a bottle of quite a decent Côtes du Rhône.

We spent the first ten minutes talking about my friend's new moustache which suited him – it made him look like a nineteenth-century Parisian artist, I said. He smiled, asked me about what I was doing. I said something vague about the writing going well, and to my relief, he didn't ask for details. We talked a bit about Picasso then, in particular his love of animals (we left the women alone). My friend suggested that had come from Picasso's love for a she-goat he'd had as a child in Malaga. I nodded, as it made sense, and I went to find the loo.

It was small and very close to our table. I had to wait till a smiling young man came out. I went in, and while peeing, noticed that the paint in the cubicle was black, and the white air-distributor on the wall sported a tiny circular sticker with *memento mori* printed on it. Nice, I thought, as I zipped up and went back to my friend.

We finished the wine, paid, and went for a walk down the canal. It was a beautiful evening, and a pleasure to be above the ground. We came to a little square overlooking a pair of locks on the canal. There was a statue there, a memorial to Frédérick Lemaître, a comedian whose dates were 1800 to 1875. There were bushes behind the statue and I saw a big rat come out of them onto the base of the statue, and run about a bit before disappearing into the undergrowth again, his tail following behind him.

We carried on and came to a beggar sitting on the street, with an upended red cap in front of him, which he picked up and held out, trembling. I normally ignored these people but today I saw the eloquence of those pleading eyes which reminded me for the first time of a punished dog – a cocker spaniel, maybe, like the one I'd had as a child. Maybe it was being in the presence of my friend that shamed me, but for once I threw a one euro coin into the cap. The man's smile humiliated me, but not as much as the note my friend threw in with the number 500 printed on it.

'You're right', I said, 'It must feel good to surprise them with what you give.'

'It might surprise him more than he realises', my friend said. 'It may look initially like a lot, but in fact it's 500 Serbian Dinars. It's worth about 4 euros.'

'That's still more than I gave', I said.

'How so? He can spend your euro. To spend mine he'd need to go to Serbia. He can't go to a Parisian bank and change the note I gave him.'

'Where the fuck did you get the Serbian banknote?'

'Ah, I had an exhibition in Novi Sad'.

He laughed and bid his adieu to me, heading off back to the Marais. I stood thinking about what he'd done. In fact,

I walked to the nearest old curved bridge over the canal and sat there on a step. Could the beggar pass it off to a half-blind shopkeeper, thinking it was a 500 euro note? I had received foreign coins in my change, but not notes. And if it did work, it might set the beggar off on a speculator's rise to riches, or relative riches anyway.

Then I turned to thinking about my friend's act. Was he trying to be nasty or to be good – or maybe just simply finding some use for the Serbian notes left over from his visit? I came to the conclusion, however, that I didn't like what he'd done. Clever, perhaps, surprising, certainly, but ultimately a bit crass. And maybe stupid, pretending to be clever. I could never condone that.

I needed to check out the goings-on in Place de la République, as several people had told me I must pay a visit. I took the Métro to République, and when I got out of the train onto the platform, a terrible stench hit my nose. It was weirdly familiar but I couldn't place it. Then I saw the man lying stretched out on the bench, his head hanging down, and I realised what it was – a decaying corpse. How had the dead man been allowed to lie there for so long?

I hurried out into the fresh air, but not before finding that the exit onto the square was blocked off, because of all the trouble, I supposed. I'd heard stories of anarchists and a heavy police crackdown, and god knows what else. This was what had made me curious to come here. I exited onto a nearby street and walked to the square.

I went straight to the famous statue of Marianne holding out an olive branch, with the inscription underneath her: *À la Gloire de la République Française.* I'd been told this was the symbol of France. I had to work to read the inscription as it was half-covered with torn posters. One of these was *Je Suis Charlie.* Of course, the Charlie Hebdo murders, an earlier flash of Islamist terrorism that we were in danger of forgetting. An interesting handwritten quote on the subject was very visible: *Dieux religions superstitions passeront – L'esprit Charlie est... immortel!* There were loads of other posters, also flowers and plants. Men and women were sitting at the base of the statue, all the way round it. The later attacks were also mourned here, needless to say, with pictures of the young people blown up in Le Bataclan on display. Several times the simple message in English *Pray for Paris* was seen on a piece of white paper underneath a grey drawing of the Eiffel Tower. And I finally saw the Latin motto that had apparently been all over Paris in the wake of the November attacks: *Fluctuat Nec Mergitur,* 'Shaken not Sunk'. A perfect motto really, and not just for Paris and its recent traumas.

I left the statue and went wandering. I passed a stall where the flag of Palestine was flying, and a couple of men were standing around, wearing green tee-shirts with Free Palestine on the front and Boycott Israel on the back. I stopped at a sign urging us all to *Marcher contre Monsanto*. Another sign read *Tailleurs de Pierre debout*. I knew 'debout' meant 'stand up', as in stand up for your rights (I could hear Bob Marley singing this in my head), and that the words in front of 'debout' referred to the building trade. I walked on.

I came to an area where a row of chairs had been laid out and facing them, a low table and a low chair. An old moustachioed man was sitting there talking into a microphone, and about twenty people were sitting listening to him intently. Oh, good, I thought, one of the anarchists. I hurried around to the back of the chairs to get a good view of him and I didn't have to listen much to see I was wrong. This was no anarchist. Behind him was a board with a line drawn down the middle, and on one side the word *pour*, on the other *contra*, with names listed underneath the words. What I'd stumbled upon was an old-fashioned debate. I quickly gathered that the subject of the debate was the use of violence in dissent – the man was speaking against the use of violence, but I could see that more people were lined up to speak in favour of the use of violence. So the spirit of debate was alive and well in France. Sadly this was not the case in Ireland.

I would have liked to sit down and hear the whole debate unfold, but sadly I realised my French wasn't up to it. I really must do something about that, I thought. My French had improved a good deal since coming here, but it was still basically shopping French – like my Romanian had been when I'd lived there. Intellectual matter would have to wait. I wandered on and came to a stall handing out free clothes for whoever wanted or needed them. Then, oddly, the next stall along was asking for stuff to be donated, clothes, hygiene things (soap, toothbrushes, combs), mobiles, hats, sleeping bags and so on – all for newly arrived migrants.

There was what might be a band sitting round a sort of tent, but no one seemed to want to start playing yet, only a young guy hammering out an insistent beat on a hand drum. The guitars lay on the ground. Then I came across a real anarchist – a young dark-haired guy with a goatee, talking very animatedly into a microphone. He was standing up, and there was a lot of people listening to him.

I'm afraid I fled. I came to something very interesting, however. It was no less than a committee against advertising. Young people all, they apparently went around defacing ads on the Métro. They had pictures of beautiful young women sellotaped to the paving stones, and were spraying slogans onto them. These seemed mainly to be urging people to object to such dehumanisations. I was reminded simultaneously of the 1960s and of the time of *La Révolution*.

I'd have to write to Monsieur Baudelaire about all this. I was sure he'd approve. I'd have to use the old name for the square as he'd have known it, however – *Place du Chateau d'Eau* and not the newer Place de la République.

I was interrupted by the arrival of a loud demo march. The crowd was large, the participants were carrying flags and pictures of a man with a moustache whom I was told was Abdullah Ocalan, the Kurdish leader, who had been imprisoned by the Turks. The flags were obviously Kurdish. There was a small police presence, but nothing too overwhelming, and the march ended peacefully enough behind the statue in the middle of the square. Where, then, was all the heaviness I'd heard about? Were the French police finally learning restraint?

I was distracted by five or six people, men and women, holding hands in a circle, and enacting a sort of slow-motion dance, where they raised their hands and lowered them. Was this tai chi? Later I saw a couple doing a more conventional South American dance in front of a group of onlookers. Unconnected to this, a group of men started tuning up their wind instruments and launched into a kind of traditional jazz. It was all go here in the Place de la République, clearly, but I needed to bid it adieu.

As I made my way to the Rue Beaurepair on the corner of the square, I saw a neat message written on a piece of paper stuck to the ground – *C'est le printemps. Je suis prêt.* This wasn't talking about the Arab Spring, I thought, or was it? If so, it would have a different meaning now.

I walked out onto the street and went to cross on a green man. Just then, a motorbike came hurtling towards me, beeping, as if it was me who'd erred. *Bastard!*, I shouted at him, but it was in the wrong language, and anyway he was gone.

I walked along Rue du Faubourg du Temple on the way to Belleville and I stopped at a shop selling rat poison. To my astonishment and my amusement, they had a window full of stuffed rats, including four small rats standing round a table, playing cards. I liked that very much. Paris was full of weird turnarounds, it seemed – poisoning and elevating the rats to art at the same time. I nearly went in and asked how much the four rats and the tiny table would cost, but I remembered I'd be going back to Ireland pretty soon, and the people at airport security might not see the joke.

It was not the first time I'd seen rat poison on sale here. Paris seemed to have a problem with rats. Someone I'd met for lunch recently had said she'd seen them running around the Métro platform when she was coming home once around midnight. I remembered a rat had made a dramatic appearance in one of Baudelaire's little poems in prose. A rich boy had lost interest in his expensive toy because he'd seen a poor boy poking a rat in an improvised cage. I'm pretty sure that wasn't an invention on Baudelaire's part – lots of poor parents probably thought of giving their children (or at least, their sons) rats as pets. Hadn't I had a pet mouse myself? The rich boy who'd seen the rat certainly was delighted at the idea of having the creature as a pet.

Many years ago a friend of mine who worked as a chef gave me his original copy of *Larousse Gastronomique* – an edition first published in the 1920s or '30s. In it was a recipe for a dish called *Cassoulet de Grand Souris*. This was basically rat meat given the *coq au vin* or *boeuf bourguignon* treatment, that is cooked in red wine with mushrooms and tiny onions. I can't remember which top Parisian restaurant introduced the dish onto their menu during the Siege of Paris in 1870 / 71, but apparently it proved very popular. It made sense too, as the Siege lasted for more than four months, and no meat was getting in, while rats were plentiful, then as now. I seem to recall the menus of the time sometimes also included rat salami, and a rat sauce called *Sauce Robert*. It's no use looking in a current edition of *Larousse* as the book has been cleaned up – all mention of rats has been removed.

I had some experience of rats when I was a child in Donegal. I commonly saw water rats swimming in the stream or small river that flowed behind my primary school. The house I grew up in had rats under the floorboards. I used to love spending time under the stairs, and sometimes the rats would come in through a hole in the back. I don't remember ever having been afraid of them but I never touched them or wanted them to walk on top of me. And I certainly never thought of capturing one and making it my pet. My little pink-eyed albino mouse was rodent enough for me, and even that was a trial for my mother.

I used to be a dog. What kind? Oh, a mongrel. Nothing poncy like the black cocker spaniel called Bonzo I had as a child. And certainly not one of those four-footed, aloof snakes that go by the name of greyhounds. I remember each and every one of the lice that lived on me.

Where did I live? In Sicily, where the sun shines like a fried egg every day of the year. I had the nose of an angel – I could smell *porcini* fifty trees away. I knew the man who would start a fight with my master the moment he walked in the bar door. I drank a saucer of red wine every day. I loved eating the butterflies that floated past me – one pounce and they were gone. And they were delicious. Better than the bones of a donkey whose meat provided salami for my master and his family. The boy was very good to me – he used to take me down to the sea and let me splash in the waves; then I'd come out onto the sand, barking, and I'd shake all the seawater onto him, wetting his clothes. He loved laughing, and I loved barking. Those were the days.

I never saw a kennel. My home was an old blanket under a gnarled vine that had been there since Dante wrote his only sestina, in homage to the troubadours. The heat was often scorching. The boy found it funny to put a straw hat on my head, one dyed in the colours of the Italian flag. I was up early, out scouting for rats to frighten away. I once peed on a hedgehog to see what it would do. I ran along the clifftop, barking at the wheeling seagulls, and at the fishing boats they flew above. I sometimes ate my master's left over spaghetti bolognaise in the taverna. My tail would wag like a fan revolving in the ceiling. I was taught party tricks that I'd be asked to do when the grappa was being downed. I'd lie on the floor and die, to great applause. I'd sit up and beg, to coos and laughter, and I'd be rewarded with a sausage – and those were sausages to swim the Adriatic for.

I'd sometimes go down to the harbour to look for an attractive grey bitch I liked the smell of. I'd have to fight off other dogs, but I was good at that. I ate one of their ears. Once I followed her onto a boat that was heading out to fill up with fish. I had to swim back and I lay on the sand and slept. When I got home my master whipped me. I ran to my blanket, whimpering.

I was once brought to a circus, and into the tent of a one-eyed woman with black hair who had a pet parrot. I barked at it, and the parrot expertly returned my bark. I lay on the multi-coloured mat and observed the strange bird who observed me. I was glad to leave that tent.

I enjoyed hearing the boy play his flute in the evenings. I heard those notes flutter up into the air, and I tried to see them, but never could. I never stopped trying, though.

The one thing I couldn't eat was cheese. The few times I tried it I vomited. On the first occasion that happened I tried to eat it again. If I got the chance now I'd manage it, I'm sure. Who would not like to be a dog in the sun? A dog in the sun, like I used to be, long ago. It was an honour.

39. SHARPSHOOTER

It had been nice to revisit the *Julien* restaurant in Rue du Faubourg St-Denis, and his American guests had admired the art nouveau lamps and the Mucha murals on the walls. They'd said nothing about the food, or the wine either, although they'd drunk enough of the latter, especially Karen. Her husband, Joss, had struck Claude as a gloomy fellow who didn't reveal much in the way of opinions, but he supposed such a make-up was necessary if one was to rise to become Deputy Secretary of Police in the Department of Homeland Security. At any rate, he doubted he would ever run into Mr and Mrs Walker again.

His wife Adelais was acting frisky, as she often did when she'd drunk a bit too much wine. It wasn't the kind of conduct befitting the partner of a high ranking officer in the SDAT, France's élite counter-terrorist task force – especially one with close ties with the Préfet de Police – Claude thought, but he said nothing. He looked out of the window, admiring the facades of the buildings they were passing.

His long-time driver Alain liked to drive fast, and had his usual contemporary jazz playing. Claude quite enjoyed the music, although he'd never asked Alain for details of what he was listening to, so he could acquire the CD and play it at home. It was not to Adelais's taste, however, and not for the first time she tried to get the music changed.

'Can you not play something with a beat, Alain, something I can sing along to?'

She laughed then, but as usual, Alain did not reply, nor did he change the music. Once when Claude had been in the car alone with him, his driver had admitted he had no other type of music anyway.

The meeting with the American policemen had got him thinking hard about the terrorist problem. In fact he wanted to kill some terrorists straight away. To Adelais's dismay, he asked Alain to make a slight detour to Avenue Foch, and the *Club de Tir* Paris, the national police shooting club. It was not far from their apartment in the Rue de la Pompe, and Adelais didn't really mind, anyway. She was never in a hurry to go home whenever they came out for a night.

The black Mercedes parked outside the club and Monsieur et Madame Durand made their way inside, Madame linking arms with Monsieur. They knew Claude in there, although he hadn't been for a month or more. He took the gun he was given, put his ear-muffs on, and went to kill the target.

The first shot missed by half a metre, the second was even worse. Claude was embarrassed, especially when Adelais collapsed in mirth alongside him.

'Oh, Claude, you're a hopeless shot. A sitting duck for any Isis terrorist with a gun.'

Was it the wine, Claude wondered? He hadn't drunk that much, certainly no more than usual. He shook his head to clear it, and called the young male assistant over.

'Would you have a target in the image of a woman? It might help my aim.'

The young man smiled, and found the kind of target he'd been asked for. Claude turned to face Adelais.

'This time I'm going to imagine the target is you', he said.

He closed his eyes and squeezed the trigger. The first shot went through the forehead of the depicted woman, the second went through her heart.

He bowed to his dear, delightful wife who had to take most of the credit for making him what he was, and brushing her hand with his lips, he said

'Madame, I bless you for my accuracy.'

40. THE STICK WITH COLOURED FEATHERS

for John Coltrane

The stick was like one dropped from heaven. It was more colourful than a rainbow. How many birds assisted its creation? How many feathers of all the colours in the spectrum had been glued to it, and what kind of glue had been used so that none of the feathers flew off and fluttered down to the ground? Had the feathers been dyed or were they the way they grew on the birds?

The man walked slowly through the busy Place de la République. He paid no attention to any of its many goings on. The red hat on his head spoke to his green shoes, his blue jacket, his white trousers. Every second step, the point of his stick jabbed the ground but all the feathers held tight. They sang to the sky. They sang to me.

I followed him at a distance like the lame boy in the story about the Pied Piper of Hamelin. But it wasn't the music of pipes I heard, it was the tenor saxophone of John Coltrane. The colours of the feathers swooped in my eyes like the archipelagos of glorious sound he created, the walks on that high tightrope stretched above silence, the silhouetted dances on the edge of the desert against the setting sun, the sure-footed striding from billow to billow on the Pacific Ocean, the waving of flags high up in the Rocky Mountains, the skateboarding on the moon. And that skateboard was multi-coloured, like the stick I followed.

I wanted it, but I knew that if I called the man and offered him all the money in my pockets, all the money in my bank account, all the money I'd ever earned, he would not sell the stick. Would I have to kill him? I could not – how could anyone kill the creator of such a magic wand? I worked at contenting myself to gaze at it, and to looking forward to remembering it when I was very old, but this was not enough. Should I jump on the man and run off with his stick, risking an intervention from the machine-gun-toting police? They might understand why I had to have it – straight line and arabesque, intention and expression, inflexibility of will, sinuosity of language, plurality of means. Just like you, John Coltrane. You said 'The music is the whole question of life itself.' In your hands, John, it was, it is. I want this stick to give to you. I salute you in immortality!

Outside the Gare Saint-Lazare, the second busiest railway station in Paris, was a stunning sculpture by the French artist Arman, a jumbled tower of clocks. Each of these clocks showed a different time, so all the time in the world was there – the choice was the viewer's, and not surprisingly then, the idea of time travel presented itself. I therefore decided on the spot I'd go back to the time of the *Pieds-Noirs*, and I'd do it by adopting a *Pied-Noir* persona.

I reasoned I needed to go back to try to make sense of the current explosive situation – to see what led up to this stand-off between the French and the violent Islamists. I knew it was a complicated issue. It was far too simplistic to connect Algeria in the 1960s and its aftermath with the actions of Isis. But that crowd would not have liked what the French did there.

I knew if I was being absolutely fair I should adopt a native Algerian persona, a Berber, but it was not my choice to have been born a white European, and I thought I'd stick with that. I sat down on the floor and had a good think about the character I was going to adopt. First of all, I decided I'd lived in Oran. My parents would have migrated to France in 1965, the second wave of the mass evacuation. This would have got me to Paris just in time for secondary school, and no doubt, two or three years of bullying. What would my name have been? How about Alex Bruel? That sounded just about right.

I decided I'd grow a moustache. And I'd buy a hat – I'd have got used to the heat in Oran. I knew I needed to prepare myself by imbibing North African culture. I'd go to Shakespeare & Co bookshop and pick up an English-language translation of one of Albert Camus's novels (probably *L'Étranger*) and maybe a translation, or better still, a recording of a performance in English, of Emmanuel Roblès's play *Montserrat*. I had a couple of jazz CDs by the

Arab composer-musicians Anouar Brahem and Ibrahim Maalouf that I could stick on, but maybe there existed a brilliant rendition of the *Pied-Noir* anthem, *Le Chant des Africains*, that I could find online and burn. Lastly there was the food – I'd read that the resettled *Pieds-Noirs*, and the other displaced Algerians, of course, had pined for the North African food they'd left behind (and not just that), so I'd have to return to that Saharan restaurant on Rue Rodier and choose a starter of *shakshuka*, served in its own little tagine, followed by a classic couscous with lamb, all washed down with Algerian red wine, of course.

I was sorted, then, apart from my French. The *Pieds-Noirs* would have had perfect French, albeit with a strong accent. In Oran it might have been spiced with a handful of Spanish words, as many of the original settlers (including Camus's mother) had been Spanish. Whatever about coming up with the latter, I'd have to live in Paris for several lifetimes to get my French good. This could be a stumbling block. At least I shared the displaced *Pied-Noir*'s discomfort of feeling removed from French culture while living here in Paris.

I thought then of the term *Pieds-Noir*. Where had it come from? I knew it had become a negative nickname given by the French natives to what they'd termed 'the French born in Algeria', but there had to be a concrete origin. I found that *Le Robert* dictionary claimed that in 1901 the term indicated a sailor working barefoot in the coal-room of a ship. Another theory had it that the name came from the black boots of French soldiers compared to the barefoot Algerians. A third explanation (that sounded like a joke) was that the *Pieds-Noirs* had arrived without their shoes, so quickly had they to leave Algeria. The last two suggestions were too mundane for me. I preferred the dirty-footed sailors. Should I get my feet dyed black, then, or at least get one of them tattooed with the words *Pied-Noir*? Would that be a bit extreme? Then, to my relief, I noticed that some of the *Pieds-Noirs*, in a spiky backlash to their pejorative nickname, had adopted as an emblem the image of two black footprints. I'd get a white tee-shirt printed with that.

As I collected these thoughts, however, I remembered the recent events here in Paris. Maybe it wasn't the *Pieds-Noirs* I should be focusing on. OK, this section of the community had experienced a bit of coldness from some quarters of the intelligentsia for their perceived exploitation of native Muslims, but so what? It was surely the massacre of hundreds of protesting Algerians (many of them hurled into the Seine from the Pont St-Michel) at a peaceful demonstration in October 1961, that I should be preoccupied with. Baudelaire seemed to be urging me to do that, as I woke up one morning with what felt like a command to go out and obtain a book of his selected art criticism. The book fell open on his piece about Fromentin's painting 'The Sleeping Arabs of Laghouat', which the painter had created weeks after seeing the streets strewn with Arab corpses. I noted the message and tried to take it on board.

It made me ask myself a question – how in hell could violence (or the memory of it) be transmitted to young men born two decades after a distant war? Did the very fact of their having Algerian parents who'd experienced that war make these young Frenchmen turn into terrorists? I didn't think so. That was far, far too easy.

So I wondered what I could now do with my *Pied-Noir* persona. I still wanted to adopt it, to shoehorn myself into the broader picture, in however weird a way. Maybe I was hoping that the reported bitterness of the *Pieds-Noirs* might have filtered down to this anti-Algerian racism that was an undeniable part of contemporary France, and was somehow reflected in their current problems. I wasn't at all sure, but I took the Métro to Abbesses in Montmartre and walked to the Rue Ravignon where the former Hôtel du Poirier once stood. It was here where Camus finished the first draft of *L'Étranger* in May 1940. It was now a block of apartments for rent, and I noticed, not without sadness and irony, there was also a mobile phone shop. When I asked some of the young people working there what they thought of Camus I was surprised by the outcome – those that had heard of him dismissed him as a colonist, a racist, and a Frenchman. He might have been amused by the last one. Or maybe not.

Double-trouble in Paris. First, two days ago, a stand-off between police and demonstrators against the new law, *la loi du travail*, that gives employers the power to hire and fire without involving the unions. The aggro all happened around the Bastille and on a march to Place de la Nation. Several arrests were made. Then yesterday, a dramatic, monsoon-like rainstorm, with thunder and lightning reinforcements that sent some people into hospital – a bunch of kids partying in a park who were daft enough to take shelter under a tree. One of them was critical, it seemed. The world was proving troublesome, indeed.

This stuff, or the new law, was what had started the business in the Place de la Republic. One had to hold it to the French for not taking government shit quietly. The Irish were unfortunately quite different on this. I wondered, was my French blood strong enough to permit me to take French nationality? I promised I would take steps to get my French fluent.

I hadn't had much contact with Monsieur Baudelaire recently. I'd gone to a poetry reading given by an American in the Shakespeare & Co bookshop that he might have liked. I'd visited an Indian vegetarian restaurant in the vicinity afterwards that he would definitely have hated. I knew Baudelaire had liked to eat good food, and drink good wine. I would have loved to cook for him – the dishes I preferred to do would not have fazed him, being mainly classic nineteenth-century French cooking. And I valued good French cheeses. Just recently, for example, I'd obtained a portion of the real Roquefort in a *fromagerie* in Rue Mouffetard – one that for the first time seemed to be that true Roquefort my friend John once told me he'd found in the tunnels there when he went wandering and was rescued by the cheese-maker's wife and brought in to taste the real stuff. Baudelaire would love that, and I think

I'd try to do *côtelettes de veau* for him, served pink, of course, and maybe accompanied by an old-fashioned but correct *ratatouille*. The only thing I'd be anxious about would be giving him a good enough wine, but then I knew I could trust him to bring at least two bottles of a wine (probably a Médoc) that would blow me away. And there was a chance he might appreciate my European jazz – there were enough accordions and trumpets in it, and suggestions of *saltimbanques*.

I was in the *Duc des Lombards* jazz club in the Les Halles district for the second performance of the evening by the featured quintet at 9.30 pm. I was seated at the drummer's left elbow, and was on my first glass of Côtes du Rhône. The band was tasty, if noticeably a bit odd. The pianist, the leader, wore a blue cap, played dementedly, and kept looking over at the super-cool, super-confident drummer, as if they had the ultimate rapport between them. The bassist was so rapt in his deft playing that he'd let a stupid look come onto his face and his tongue push out between his lips. The trumpeter and the saxophonist, when they weren't rasping out notes, kept laughing at the antics of the other three. When the trumpet was being blown I saw drops of spit falling from its end – once the musician took off the mouthpiece and emptied out what had accumulated. The instrument fell once and the leader made a joke that the trumpet was broken now, so the audience could leave, getting a full refund at the ticket desk.

I was greatly enjoying the playing when I noticed on the TV screens that showed the band from different angles someone I recognised. It was Denis Ackroyd! God, I hadn't seen him in twenty years! What was he doing in Paris? Ackroyd was an artist, a painter I'd collaborated a bit with in the early '90s. He'd been born and brought up in Cornwall, I think, but was then living in London, as I was. My publisher of the time had brought us together. I remembered attending one of his openings in a trendy gallery in Cork Street. Denis was dressed completely in black, as was his wife and most of the assembled gathering. I was uncool in a blue denim get-up. Not long after that, I recalled, Denis had an exhibition in LA, and he'd spent a week or two there, and told me later that LA was the coolest place in the universe. I still hadn't been there.

Now here he was on the little television screen. I had to

go over and accost him. He recognised me instantly and appeared pleased to see me. It was too noisy, however, to talk, so we agreed to catch up later. I went back to my seat with one more glass of wine, and enjoyed the rest of the set.

The band was barely off the stage when he was standing in front of me. He was suggesting, if I was in no hurry, that we decamp to a wine-bar he liked in the *quartier* of Belleville where he was living. It was a Friday night, and I'd been happy to bump into him again, so agreed to accompany him. It was not that far from where I was staying.

Predictably, it was a cool wine-bar. There were more wines in there than in any off-license I'd ever been in. All were available by the glass, although I didn't think this would concern us. I let Denis choose the wine and he didn't disappoint me. He quickly let me know that his marriage had broken up a long time ago, and a second one had broken up since then. He was solo now. And his art had changed too. I remembered his paintings as being very charming, and I don't mean this as a put-down. They were abstract, with a strong emphasis on colours, and a bit of interest in geometry. He astonished me, as he filled my glass with the second dishing-out of his excellent St-Émilion, by telling me his recent work had included human figures. Well, one human figure, he clarified – a remarkable-looking boy.

I was immediately intrigued. Had my old friend been hiding a pederast inclination? I threw that crude thought out of my head and waited to be enlightened. This is the story I was told:

'As a professional painter I began to feel my art was lacking a great deal by excluding the human form. I mean, there I was, walking around, looking closely at the features and faces of the people I met, or even passed, and getting pleasure from it. This faculty was enhancing my life, I had no doubt of it, so why was I keeping it from my work? The thought remained in the abstract until one day I was walking around the Saint-Denis district, and I laid eyes on a beautiful boy. He was cheeky, and fiery looking, provocative, even. I knew straight away I had to paint him. This was the one.

His parents were of North-African origin and spoke limited French, but we got by. They were fine with the boy coming to my studio to pose for me, especially when I suggested a sum of money they were happy with. I smuggled his likeness onto a number of canvasses, not going anywhere near a full or even partial portrait, but he burned out from all of these paintings. And he was different in each of them – one time looking like a gypsy, another time a killer; once a rent-boy, then an angel, or (my favourite) the most soulful singer in a choir. His ways were very funny too. I was enjoying having him around. I also couldn't wait to open an exhibition of these paintings. They might make my name.

So one day when I went to collect him I took a huge chance and asked the parents if I could borrow the boy, have him come to stay with me for an indefinite length of time. I knew he had to back at school at the end of summer, but it was the start of summer now. The idea was (as I told them) that I wanted to push hard for a big exhibition, and work over the next month or two as if my days on earth were limited. It took a long time to go to Saint-Denis to get him, and again to take him back – time I could channel into my work, I said. I'd made sure to bring a bunch of flowers for the mother and a box of the best Medjool dates for the father. They invited me to drink some mint tea with them, and asked me questions about what their son would be doing. I explained he wouldn't have to do much – run errands, clean my brushes, pose, as before. I would give him pocket money for these little tasks, and I'd buy him clothes. They seemed satisfied, especially the mother. I think she thought I'd teach the lad how to paint. Maybe, if he showed any interest or inclination, I would.

So I brought the boy to Belleville. I had quite a big studio there (that was why I took up residence in that area, where property was cheaper), which was on the top floor and very bright – as well as a couple of big windows, there was a skylight I loved, and had put in as soon as I moved there. The boy liked staying in the studio. It was much better than living in the cramped, impoverished flat in Saint-Denis, he said, and I think he came to enjoy seeing his face in the paintings. It's only when one lives with someone that one gets to really know them, however, and I discovered that my beautiful boy was very moody indeed. In fact, I'd never seen anyone get as sad as he did from time to time. There was no shaking him out of that state when he fell into it, but it didn't usually last too long. Only once was he completely gone from me for two whole days and I can tell you I was slightly scared. I had no idea what brought on these states, if anything. I knew, though, it was nothing to do with his being separated from his parents.

I discovered something else very soon. The boy had developed a passion for sweet things. I didn't mind too much my fancy bars of Swiss chocolate disappearing, but my gradually emptying bottles of sweet, alcoholic liqueurs was another matter. And, ridiculous as it might sound, I began to think he was taking my carefully hidden cocaine. I got stroppy with him one day and threatened to return him to his parents. I noticed some improvement after that, but then I had to take the train to Brussels for an exhibition that was happening there, and I knew I'd be away for some time. I left the boy enough food, of course (and plenty of chocolate) and he didn't seem to mind my going. I took my cocaine with me.

I got back to a terrible shock, the worst I've ever experienced in my life. The boy was hanging from a cup-hook screwed into the bathroom door. He'd used my judo belt. The smell in the studio was awful – I ran to open all the windows. His feet didn't quite meet the ground and a chair, which no doubt he'd kicked away, lay nearby. His head had dropped onto his shoulder, and the face was swollen, and blue, and barely recognisable. The eyes stared at me, making me look away.

With great difficulty, I cut him down. I had to hold him up with one arm, while attempting to sever the judo belt with a knife that wasn't sharp enough. Finally, I managed it, and laid the body on a divan. I looked at it, and I tell you, I cried a bucket-load of tears.

I called a doctor who advised me to summon a policeman. The doctor told me the boy had been dead for days, and that *rigor mortis* was well set-in. We needed scissors to remove the clothes for burial. The policeman was more than suspicious – I think the fact that I was a foreigner and a single artist played a part, but I also got the idea that the fact the boy was of Arab stock was to my benefit. All I knew was I didn't trust him.

One huge task remained to be done, and I loathed the idea. I had to go round to the boy's parents and tell them what had happened. Somehow my feet took me there. To my astonishment, the mother was unmoved. I put this weird response down to the horror of what she was taking on board. My granny used to tell me that the worst suffering happened in silence. As for the father, he seemed to be in a world of his own, and said only 'Perhaps it was for the best: he was heading for a fall.'

I went back to deal with the removal of the corpse, having enlisted the help of a trusted friend. As we were finishing our preparations, the doorbell rang and I was astonished to be confronted by the boy's mother. She said she wanted to see her son's body. Of course, I let her in – it was not for me to decree what was right or not, and anyway I felt guilty. I would not have been surprised if she'd brought a small axe out of her bag and brought it down on my head.

She asked me to show her where the act had occurred, and I was not inclined to do this, but as my eyes swivelled to the bathroom door I saw that the cup-hook and the remains of the judo-belt were still hanging there. I jumped out of my chair to pull the evidence of the tragedy out of the door and put them in the bin, but the poor woman grabbed my arm and pleaded with me to give them to her. I was convinced her son's death had sent her over the edge and she was full of tender feelings for the instruments of her son's death, which she wanted to preserve as dark relics. I gave her what she wanted.

There followed the attempt to get back to normal work, and rid from my mind the ghost who was staring down at me from the bathroom door. I went back to abstract work. The letters, though, started to come in, mostly from people I didn't know. Some were jokey, apparently, some were bordering on the illiterate, in a pretentious, arty way, but they all had one purpose: to extract from me a piece of the fatal, blessed judo belt. I have to say one more thing – I could see all these letters were from the more affluent section of society, and the majority were from women. There was no letter written in Arabic.

I suddenly saw why the mother had wanted the judo-belt and the cup-hook, and what consoling trade it was she planned.'

I was shocked to see that, in a French railway station, the lost property office was called *Objets Trouvés*, or 'found objects'. Made sense, really. The news this morning was not to do with France. It was far away in Cincinnati, USA, where a male gorilla called Harambe was shot dead because a 4-year-old boy had fallen into his enclosure at the zoo. Apparently, anger was mounting at the shooting. I wondered what Monsieur Baudelaire would have had to say.

Had he ever gone to a zoo? There is evidence in his writing (in the prose-poems at least) that he liked animals. He could not have visited the Paris Zoo in Bois de Vincennes, as it only opened in 1934. He could, however, have gone to the *Jardin des Plantes* where animals from King Louis XIV's menagerie at Versailles had been transplanted. He might also have paid a trip to London Zoo, or the famous *Tiergarten Schönbrunn* in Vienna. In fact, he did visit all three, I've decided, and he wrote a triptych prose-poem on the subject which he called 'Three Zoos', and which has gone missing. I should visit all the lost property offices in France, although I seriously doubted the poem would be among the Objets Trouvés. It was too far back in time. No, the only option was for me to write the prose-poem myself and pretend it was Baudelaire's – I'd make sure to have at least one gorilla in it, also a panther, as a nod to a later poet who'd resided in Paris. I couldn't write the poem in French, obviously, but I could write it in English and inveigle a French poet to translate it, sounding a bit old. I knew just the poet – she'd already translated from the English, and could be relied on to keep stumm, and even enjoy the little joke. Then I could translate the lost but found Baudelaire poem into English and send it to *The TLS*. Everybody would be happy then, except maybe Monsieur Baudelaire.

'Wow, imagine finding you here in *La Goutte d'Or*! You of all people, renowned baker of the trendiest manna, renouncer of the sexiest devils in the urban wastelands. What do you hope to find in this *quartier*?'

'Listen, you know I hate designer shops and car-clogged boulevards – give me the desert any day. Even here the traffic is lethal. I had literally to jump to avoid a speeding black van while crossing the street, and in the process my halo fell off, right down among the litter and dog-shit on the edge of the pavement. The crowd rushing by wasn't stopping, so I decided it was safer to let my head-insignia lie there. Anyway, I suddenly felt freer. Felt that maybe now I could do things I never allowed myself to do – truly bad things, you know. I can be like you. I've had it up to here with being well-behaved.'

'I hope you at least alerted the police to your loss. Or put a note up in the nearest Objets Trouvés?'

'None of those things. I've decided I like it here. There's no pressure on me. I enjoy the fact that most of the people around me here are of a different religion to me. I have nothing against Moslems. And you're the only person who's recognised me, which suits me perfectly. Do you live around here? We could go to *Le marché Dejean* and shop, then go back to your place and let me cook a very hot chilli. There must be a decent wine-shop. Maybe we might end up in a cool bar?'

'What if someone finds your halo and puts it on?'

'Oh, nobody would believe in it. They would just think it was some kind of weird headgear. Only maybe a third-rate poet would pick it up and put it on, then wish the Nobel Prize for him- or herself – and you know something, I would love that, it would make me laugh louder that I've ever laughed before. I can just think of the poets I want to find it. Hey, let's go to a bar straight away.'

I'm not a doctor. I have an old friend in Berlin who is one, and I'm friendly with my own doctor in Donegal, but I'm a writer. Not of much use to society, really. Yet one night when I was walking back home down Boulevard de Clichy, en route to Rue des Martyrs, I was accosted by a young woman who put her arm through mine and asked if I was a doctor. 'Certainly not', I said, 'I'm very sorry.'

I appraised her. She was tall, and not especially pretty. Was slightly dark-skinned, clearly of North African extraction, and not too made-up. She was well enough dressed.

'Yes, you are a doctor', she said, switching to English. 'I'd know one at a glance. Come home with me.'

'I might come to see you, after you've found a doctor.'

'You're funny, you are. I've met others like you, but you're the best. Come, let's go.'

I was mildly intrigued, that's the only way I can explain it, but I allowed myself to be led away. I was not remotely interested in her sexually, or that's what I told myself. Her English was unusually good for a Parisian, and it didn't sound American, so I suspected she'd spent time in Britain.

We came to a street called Rue Darcet, just after Place de Clichy, where we went upstairs to a squalid little apartment. It was hardly an apartment, more a bedsit. I was surprised, however, to see three reproductions of what seemed to be portraits of eminent doctors hanging on her wall.

She opened a bottle of quite a decent Burgundy, and offered me a cigar, which I declined. Undeterred, she lit one for herself and helped me with the wine.

'Make yourself at home', she said, 'And allow yourself to float back to when you were a young intern. You had no grey in your beard then. I remember you well, coming out of serious operations, flushed with having handed that great surgeon his instruments – I forget his name. There was a man who loved to cut, snip and trim! You were in awe of his ability to do amazing things in such a short amount of time. Admit it, my sweet. You are a doctor.'

'I certainly am not.'

'I'll prove it', she said.

She took a bundle of papers from a cupboard, photocopies of old headshots of famous surgeons that we all might have heard of. She pointed to one and asked me if I recognised him.

I said I did – his name was written on the bottom of it, but I'd actually met him at a dinner-party in Hampstead in the mid '70s.

'Aha', she said, 'I knew you were a doctor. And this fellow is another surgeon who called your acquaintance a monster who wears his black soul on his face. Why? Because they disagreed on a diagnosis, and the patient died. This other one', she said, pointing to a third headshot, 'gave the names of the left-wing protesters he was treating in the hospital to the police. It was the time of the rioting. He looks too nice, doesn't he, to have been so treacherous? I saw him once when he gave a talk at the Sorbonne.'

She then removed a large brown envelope from a drawer, and withdrew half a dozen or so black and white photographs. They all showed young doctors working as interns but none of them looked remotely like me. To my surprise, she didn't try to claim one of them did.

'When we next meet I hope you'll give me your photograph', she said.

'Why do you think I'm a doctor?' I asked.

'Because you're so good and kind to women.'

'That's daft logic', I said, but the word 'daft' puzzled her. I tried 'bizarre'.

'Oh, I've been proved right many times. I've known many doctors. I love them so much I go to see them when there's nothing wrong with me.'

'And how do they react?'

'Sometimes they see straight away there's nothing wrong with me, and ask me to leave. But others are kinder. They sympathise, and I slip 10 euros onto their desk. Once in the Pitié-Salpêtrière Hospital I came across a young intern, so handsome, polite and hard-working. I gathered from a couple of his colleagues that he was broke, so I invited him to come and see me as often as he liked, and ask for whatever he wanted. I told him I didn't need money. I conveyed this to him indirectly. I have a fantasy, you see. I'd love him to turn up with his surgical instruments, and his white coat all bloody.'

I was told this very frankly, as if it were a normal admission.

'When did this obsession start?' I asked.

'I don't know... I can't remember' she said, turning her eyes to the floor.

I made my excuses about the hour being late, and got up to go. I thanked her for the wine and the conversation, and made my way down to the street. The sad people that are loose in the world, I thought. If there's a God there, why doesn't he protect them? I was given the taste for horror so I could stand the world, as a knife leads to healing. Is there such a thing as an innocent monster? All mad people should be protected. Who is to say why some of us exist, and why some of us might have been better served by not having come into existence.

47. RAIN

'Ô le chant de la pluie!' – PAUL VERLAINE

This May in Paris has been the wettest since 1853. Just my luck to have chosen this month to live here. And what the rain was doing to the city! Yesterday at least the rain had stopped and I went walking in the region of the Eiffel Tower (whose tip was surrealistically invisible in a cloud). I was going along the Quai d'Orsy and could see the Seine had flooded. The walkways on the riverbank were underwater – so much for the famous Paris *plage*. I saw tables and chairs half-submerged, as were lampposts. Broken-off bits of trees were afloat in the water, which looked brown and muddy. The old *bateaux mouches* kept moored to the banks as floating restaurants were drifting in the centre of the river. What would Baudelaire have made of his native city?

I stopped at a kiosk and bought a copy of *Le Figaro*. Yes, I was aware of what I was doing, and I hoped nobody I knew had seen me make my purchase, but sometimes it's good to be aware of the right-wing angle on current events. I found a café and ordered an espresso.

The paper did not disappoint me. The headline shrieked *Grèves, violence: l'image de la France se dégrade.* More rain! And it got worse further down the front page where the editorial was titled *Un pays du temps jadis*, a country of the past. The metaphor that followed fleshed out this verdict – an old nation crippled with rheumatism, huddled over its archaisms and acquired rights, incapable of modernising itself. Without a future, or horizon. That was telling it! Then came the reasons – 'It says a lot about our state of decay, about this France where you can attack a police car with an iron bar, where an old-guard union with a Marxist ideology can stop trains, metros, ports, airports and refineries, where the repeated demonstrations can degenerate into pitched battles between the police and the people. It says a lot about this France where an active sectarian minority is imposing its will. Does the plane have a pilot anymore?'

I read this with interest and, I'm afraid to say, some agreement, and I have never been remotely right-wing. Maybe I needed to rethink my earlier interest in taking out French nationality. *Does the plane have a pilot anymore?* Well, Charles, from what I've told you, what do you think? How does it match with the France you knew? I had intended putting the newspaper in the bin, but I tore off the front page, folded it and put it in my pocket. I decided to go home before the city went underwater, before the Métro tunnels flooded.

When I got back and checked my email, I saw that my friend who was to travel from Basel to meet me for dinner on my last evening in Paris tomorrow wasn't coming. His train had been cancelled because of the strike. The old-guard unions had rained on his plans.

Some people who are wholly contemplative and unsuited to action can still behave in a way they would never have expected. For example, which of us has not, on occasion, dreaded bad news, and stayed up all night pacing the floor? Or left mail unopened because we fear what it might contain? Or delay dealing with a matter that is way overdue, because we hate the idea of it? Is it some mysterious force, known to the Incas or other Indians, that dictates our actions? No doctor can explain such compulsions, or the madness to perform absurd and dangerous acts.

I once knew a man, for example, who lived in a squat in East London. I used to visit him in winter, and for warmth he kept pulling up floorboards and burning them, while his living area shrank. I pointed this existential problem out to him, but he laughed, pulled another board up, and flung it on the fire. I left him and never visited him again.

Another person I knew used to love smoking cigarettes next to a petrol tank, and chortle when he flung the butts down into the petrol-puddles on the ground.

This kind of weird, sporadic energy and lack of foresight comes from ennui and low esteem, I know. And sometimes from the smoking of marijuana. These people need something to fill up their time. They spend too long floating in one or other kind of reverie.

And there are people so fearful they hesitate to enter a café, or queue up at a theatre box-office. They might feel inferior to the confident staff working there. It could be due to the fact they don't feel they're attractive enough. Or maybe there's no reason at all.

I have often felt a victim to such lethargy, such a lack of belief that I have anything to offer. That's when I think some demon has got inside of me, and is working to make me fulfil his wishes.

I heard some pleasant oud music out on the street one morning, for example. It was beautifully relaxing so I opened the French windows and went onto the balcony. I saw a child musician walking in front of an older Arab man who was carrying a number of rugs. *Un tapis perse, de très bonne qualité,* was what he was singing, in some kind of time with the music. He looked laden, like a Spanish mule. It was a long time since a carpet salesman had hawked his cloth down Rue Rodier, I reckoned, and never with such ceremony. Nevertheless, I found myself taking against the fellow. I yelled down at him to come up. I had to shout twice the code he needed to get through the front door.

I lived on the fourth floor, and the lift had been out of order for weeks, but it was operational again now. I wouldn't have minded him carrying the rugs up the stairs. He arrived, sweating, anyway, and I brought him in, asking to see his wares. He spread them on the floor, one by one – he had about six and they weren't very big. I sat watching, with my lip turned up like an Inca cacique. When he'd finished, I said:

'Not a lot of colour or pattern, is there? Are you sure they're Persian? Are they made of sheep's wool at all, not to mention the *kurk* wool that comes from the sheep's neck? They're far from an Istahan carpet, or an Ushag rug – where's the brick-red background? In fact, I'd bet the fabric, or at least the dye, contains some synthetic ingredients. Why are you trying to trick me?'

I ushered him out the door and he went, cursing, and I heard him muttering as he waited for the lift. Meanwhile I opened a bottle of cheap wine which I'd intended for cooking a *boeuf bourguignon* and went out to wait for him on the balcony. The Arab boy with the oud was waiting patiently for his father. I wished him no harm, but when the carpet-seller emerged I poured all the wine down all over his rugs, making sure to shake the bottle, so the splatters spread.

'Next time come up with some quality', I roared. 'Life has to be made beautiful.'

And I knew I would suffer for such antics, but what does the threat of hellfire, however literal, matter to someone who has known such short-timed but absolutely genuine joy?

A metaphor for life? How about a hospital ward. I'm suffering by the radiators and I think if I swapped beds with you, by the window, I'd recover in a week.

As the singer had it, the other man's grass is always greener. It was Dusty Springfield, wasn't it? Recently I've got fed up with a new Paris habit – men pulling out their dicks and blatantly peeing in the streets. It's the tiny things that always make us snap and demand a change. I don't think I have a soul but if I had one it would be time for a discussion with him. I know I have an unconscious, so I could always interrogate that being (as I tend to do in my writing, anyway). I want to ask him / them where I might move to if I had to get out of this city.

How about Lisbon? I've been there once – in fact, I was delayed a week by the Icelandic volcanic cloud. The sun shines, the Duoro wines are good, there's excellent fish to eat (as long as one doesn't overdo it). The little yellow trams zip recklessly up the hill to Alfama, bells ringing. Ghosts abound, including Pessoa's. The *fado* music makes one sad one hasn't died.

No response from my unconscious, or my soul, if he's there.

Maybe Berlin is another option? I lived there and got to love the city. My favourite bit was Kreuzberg. The language is beautiful to my ears. It's cheaper than Paris, and even better for art, although that must be hard to believe. Next time you go there, treat yourself and pay a visit to the *Alte National Galerie* on the Museumsinsel, and spend an hour in the Casper David Friedrich room, where you'll see that Germany was the home of Romanticism.

Still no reply from the two boys. They love staying in hiding.

What about Mexico? It's far enough away, and their Aztec past is dark, but colourful – and they have a magnificent museum to show this. The food is fantastic, too (though it's hard to get decent Mexican food outside the country). They even have some decent wine, made in Baja California. And the plangency of the mariachi music that has influenced American rock music so much!

Still not a sound from the pair. The soul clearly doesn't exist, then, and the unconscious is shy.

I up the ante. How about Greenland, then? They eat sautéed seals' eyeballs there. Or Japan – the island of Hokaiddo, maybe, with its earthquakes and volcanoes? Or let's go all the way down to the Antarctic and have a dance with the penguins? The light must be marvellous there. Or maybe not quite so far south – Tasmania, and hunt for its extinct tigers? Is the devil making these suggestions?

Finally I get a very loud, choral reply (so there is a soul, clearly): 'Anywhere, as long as it's out of this world.'

I have a bit of a wooden face this morning – *gueule de bois*, the colourful French term for a hangover. Even the word for face that's used has an animal ring to it, so it's half a horse or a half-bear that's saying cheerio to you, Charles. It's been extremely good spending time with you, and exchanging ideas. I know you're out of this world, literally speaking, but when I read your prose poems and do my *flâneur* bit through the streets of Paris, I feel you're still partially here. When I was saying my farewell to your city last night, I poured one glass of the quite decent Bordeaux out for you, Charles, and when I came back from the toilet I was glad to see the glass empty. I hope the wine was acceptable.

I don't know when, *mon ami*, but I will return here, to spend more time. That seems to have been the way with writers and artists – one taste of Paris leads to a desire to taste it again. Next time I come, I want to get closer to you, bring you into this world a bit more. I could start with organising a séance and trying to contact you directly. Right on top of your grave in Montparnasse would be good, but I wonder how easy it would be to slip into the cemetery at night. I foresee another difficulty – one friend I would want to accompany me is a dramatist who admires you, and who never goes anywhere without her dog. Dogs are not allowed in Paris cemeteries (though most have wild cats living in them). But even a good contact via a séance would not be enough. No, I'd want you to be corporally here next time. I'd like to take you to the *Duc des Lombards* jazz club and see what you'd make of jazz – maybe that German guitar ace, Ulf Wakenius, would be playing there again (I'd heard him say it was his favourite jazz joint in Paris). Or to the cinema to see a Jim Jarmusch film, maybe a new one he'd just have released. Oh, I'd like to do many interesting things with you, and sit in the front row at your first poetry reading in a hundred and fifty years – they would never find a hall big enough to hold the audience that would come for that. Not even the Stade de France would do. With all this transhumanism stuff that's in vogue, as well as all the medical research that's multiplying all the time, maybe they'll finally find a way to bring people back from the dead – not just anybody or everybody, just a few very special people that would have earned their right to return. Would some of those devil friends of yours not be able to help? Anyway, I'll leave it there, Charles. I'm not saying *adieu* but *au revoir*.

Ton ami, le deuxième, moindre Rôdeur parisien.

Born in Donegal in 1952, Matthew Sweeney settled in Cork, having previously lived in Berlin, Timişoara, Romania and, for a long time, London.

Elected a member of Aosdána, Sweeney produced numerous collections of poetry for which he won several awards, including the Prudence Farmer Prize, the Cholmondeley Award and a T. S. Eliot Prize short-listing (for *Black Moon*). His novels for children include *The Snow Vulture* (1992) and *Fox* (2002).

His most recent poetry collections, all from Bloodaxe, were *My Life as a Painter* (2018), *Inquisition Lane* (2015) and *Horse Music* (2013) which won the inaugural Piggott Poetry Prize.

His poetry has appeared widely in poetry magazines and has been translated into Dutch, German, Italian, Japanese, Mexican Spanish, Romanian and Slovakian. A full-length collection, *Hund und Mond*, translated into German by the poet Jan Wagner, was published by Hanser Berlin in September 2017.

He collaborated twice with the English poet, John Hartley Williams – first in the handbook, *Writing Poetry* (1996), then in the satirical novel, *Death Comes for the Poets* (2013). He also edited or co-edited several poetry anthologies.

Matthew Sweeney died in Cork of motor neurone disease in August 2018.